Reaching foı   --ı

Alan Brunskill Webster was born in 1918 and has served the Church of England as a curate and youth leader in the east end of Sheffield, as a teacher at Westcott House and Lincoln Theological College, as vicar of Barnard Castle, and as Dean of Norwich and of St Paul's. He was a member of the General Synod and of the Crown Appointments Commission. He has shared in many of the fresh initiatives of twentieth-century Christianity, including co-operative work between churches, the campaign against investment in apartheid South Africa, and the foundation of Cathedral Camps and of lay consultative bodies to democratize cathedrals. His concerns have also included the ordination of women as priests, the creation of the Norwich Night Shelter, and the *Faith in the City* report. He and his wife Margaret have two daughters and two sons, and they live in Norfolk.

For our grandchildren
Cofi, Chanice, Jonathan,
William and Lorenzo

Reaching for Reality

Sketches from the Life of the Church

ALAN WEBSTER

Published in Great Britain in 2002 by
Society for Promoting Christian Knowledge
Holy Trinity Church
Marylebone Road
London NW1 4DU

Biblical quotations marked NJB are from the New Jerusalem Bible,
published and copyright © 1985 by Darton, Longman & Todd Ltd and
Doubleday, a division of Random House, Inc., and used by permission.
Biblical quotations marked REB are from the Revised English Bible © 1989
Oxford University Press and Cambridge University Press.
Biblical quotations marked AV are from the Authorized Version of the
Bible (The King James Bible), the rights of which are vested in the Crown,
and are reproduced by permission of the Crown's Patentee, Cambridge
University Press.
Biblical quotations marked RSV are from the Revised Standard Version ©
1946, 1952 and 1971, by the Division of Christian Education of the
National Council of the Churches of Christ in the United States of
America. Used by permission. All rights reserved.

British Library Cataloguing-in-Publication Data

A catalogue record for this book is available from the British Library

ISBN 0–281–05438–X

Typeset by Pioneer Associates, Perthshire
Printed in Great Britain by
Antony Rowe Ltd., Chippenham, Wiltshire

CONTENTS

FOREWORD

Emerging, as it were, from the last pages of this remarkable book I felt like someone walking from the colourful darkness of a glorious cathedral into brilliant sunlight. While my love of art and history remained informed by all that I had encountered within it, I found myself being wonderfully reminded of all that brightness which cannot be contained by creeds and statutes, and which, officially, has made Faith such a difficult thing to handle. Apologias for the Church abound. It has in its long day been everything from a cruel to an embarrassing institution, making many a Christian life a misery. Its tanglings with the state all over the world at various times, some very recent, have disgraced it. And then, as now, someone comes along who has an authority to speak up for its true heart and soul, and to be its proper remembrancer, and to say, as Alan Webster does, what it really is. For nothing else is so often forgotten, and frequently by churchmen themselves – though never by those myriad worshippers who would find it impossible to discover words for what they know of Christ. Not that Alan Webster shows us two Churches, one official the other spiritual. What we see through the lives of those individuals chosen by him as exemplars of what Christianity means is the ceaseless nourishing of an ancient institution by those who are still willing to die for what it really declares. All the people he names, some centuries ago, many just the other day, have reached out to grasp Christ's meaning, often to their peril.

The last century was both the most appalling and most scientifically progressive in human history. It made great strides, it made epic suffering and countless martyrs. It should have raised a total disbelief in the existence of a loving God. Its barbarity was filmed from start to finish and there is no more shocking archive to be found. We stare at the footage with horror. Where, we ask, was the Lord in all this? Where was he in the delicate business of the Falklands service in St Paul's? How was it that Julian managed to find him in the grim Norwich of her day, with its Lollards' pit and plague? Dietrich Bonhoeffer, kneeling naked at the foot of the gallows, knew that he was by his side. Less terribly, many a country parson struggling with poverty, sickness and ignorance in some remote parish in earlier times, would find his bishop the major hindrance to his ministry. Alan Webster's grandfather was such a priest. He analyses the quaint term 'cure of souls' and gives a vivid account of how a woman priest more than just coped with the 13 parishes she was given, how she and just a handful of their 3,000 inhabitants kept the Church alive, and how she was far from alone in doing this.

Reaching for Reality is an autobiographical journey. Its views are passionate and radical but also wise and balanced. It will take readers through their own times, constantly reminding them of their profoundly religious nature – just in case they might think of themselves as living in a post-Christian world. A differently Christian world, perhaps – but then the Church's past, the real Church's past, is often another tale to that told by theologians. It is our knowledge (or suspicion) of this which keeps Faith so fresh and exciting. Alan Webster reveals the Church's debt to its poets, the timeless words of George Herbert, the language of the hymn writers, and, very dear to him, that of the Psalmist.

One of the most important aspects of this excellent book is its personal encounter with both the rural and city Church, and how Alan Webster possessed views which he knew would be challenged in either. At Norwich and St Paul's Cathedrals he was able to bring with him a warm democratic culture which enhanced their beautiful stately functions, and beauty itself he sees as part of that 'reality' which is the goal of those who seek to live in the presence of Christ. Among the many values of *Reaching for Reality* are its perceptive reminders of so many recent happenings, everything from the martyrdom of Oscar Romero to the new liturgy and the ordination of women. The cure of souls has in his lifetime taken many turns, and none of us are what we were even twenty years ago. Sensitive and intelligent, Alan Webster has a necessary and fascinating story to tell. He allows it to unwind from his own existence – his own soul, whilst recognizing that there is no end to it. Nothing lasts except the Church, said George Herbert.

Ronald Blythe

INTRODUCTION

These pages describe occasions when religious life has been realigned after it had drifted away from reality. The religious traditions, inherited by the Christian churches, have flashes of change. The churches break out of routines and free themselves from words which no longer resonate and customs which no longer serve the gospel. Their members experience resurrection. All these events have been costly, not cheap; they all involve risks. Often the risk-takers have been criticized for crossing frontiers. But these flashes of change show that religion, to the surprise of some, has not become fossilized but continues to live and develop. Secularization in western society has not led to God's funeral.

I have taken many of my instances from the Church of England, simply because it has been my primary pathway, though friends in other churches or in none have taught me much. Other faiths have also been experiencing fresh life, and they all have gifts to offer to humanity. Globalization and advances in technology require world faiths to pause and consider how they can best contribute together to a compassionate human existence in the world of our new century. All will have to risk change and recognize their own wells of hope.

Very often new light dawns after a pause. At the church of St Merri in Paris, surrounded by the crowds which are drawn to the Centre Pompidou, I asked the priests how they arrived at the inspired liturgy, exhibitions, hospitality and welcoming prayers at their church. They replied, 'When we came here it was essential for a year to do absolutely nothing.'

'But you must have had services?'

'Non, rien, absolument rien!'

In their waiting, they were granted resurrection.

Within the Church's search for truth in word and deed stands the figure of Jesus Christ, so radical, elusive and powerful. His story and his presence continue to inspire and surprise. He refuses to be neatly classified or convincingly explained. In the Gospels each generation discovers new truths. We cannot do better in the twenty-first century than apply to him those Old Testament words which were reaching for the divine reality:

> This is only a fraction of what he has done
> and all we catch of it is the feeblest echo.
> But who can conceive the thunder of his power?
> (Job 26.14, NJB)

I am indebted to many friends and colleagues whose names appear as sources. I also acknowledge the expert assistance of those who have helped prepare the script: Pauline Druiff, David Edmunds, Pat Bartlett, and Ruth McCurry acting as editor on behalf of SPCK. I especially would like to thank Ronald Blythe for his Foreword. Others who have shown much generosity include: Andrew Anderson, Humphrey Cranfield and Bert Richards (Chairman of that growing ecumenical body the Norfolk Theological Society), who read the text and was, as always, alert, witty and helpful. I am grateful to the Librarians of St Paul's and Norwich Cathedral. In particular I am aware of the support of Alison, John, Stephen and Catherine, who have borne with me, sustained and enlivened me. And special thanks must go to Margaret, without whose creativity and encouragement I could not have carried through this enterprise.

Alan Webster

1 CURE OF SOULS: Changing and Unchanging

But thou wilt sin and grief destroy;
That so the broken bones may joy
And tune together in a well set song
Full of his praises
Who dead men raises
Fractures well cured make us more strong.

(George Herbert)

The metaphors used in the language of Christianity include the surprising phrase 'cure of souls'. This points to a mysterious task of considering our relationships and keeping our imagination alert. If our own and each other's souls are to be cared for then we need to be sensitively related with each other. Some believe that the 'soul' is an entity distinct from our bodies; others that it is the centre of our personality and of our relationships with God and each other. In the Church of Scotland the metaphors for ministry and especially for 'the charge' which is given to the newly appointed are pastoral. Though many might not use the phrase 'cure of souls', the aim is at the heart of the modern teaching, health, social and counselling services. 'Cure' in the phrase 'cure of souls' simply means 'care' as in the word 'care-taker'.

The Anglican pastoral tradition was famously set out in the life, poems and essays of the seventeenth-century priest, pastor, poet and musician, George Herbert. Living shortly before civil war disrupted the society in which he was born, he understood that suffering must be shared and mutual understanding fostered – the courage to give nothing less than life itself was needed if the deep wounds were to be healed. He saw his role as being constantly available to his parishioners, supporting them in dark days. He was a musician, never happier than when he could say to his friends: 'Let us tune our instruments'. He kept rudimentary medical supplies. The worship held in Bemerton village church always spoke of hope and resurrection.

Barnard Castle

The phrase 'cure of souls' is still used whenever a new vicar starts work. On 21 February 1953 I knelt before Michael Ramsey, then Bishop of Durham, afterwards Archbishop of Canterbury, on being appointed vicar of Barnard Castle, a north-country town of 5,000 people in Teesdale. 'Receive the cure of souls which is mine and thine' were his words. He looked searchingly into my eyes as though he was questioning as well as commissioning. R. S. Thomas, the Welsh poet-priest, in 'The Empty Church', has reflected on the ambiguity of the task of the cure of souls for those commissioned to perform it. He hoped that in some mysterious way 'someone greater than I can understand' would be revealed within the church.

From the walls of the dark sandstone church of Barnard Castle, carved medieval faces looked down reminding us that we were members of a centuries-old community of faith in that dale, with a history of religious conflict: fighting at the Rising of the North, and violence during John Wesley's open-air preaching, the fire engine (kept in the parish church) dousing the preacher.

About 200 people were silently watching the Bishop. A farmer churchwarden stood at the front with head bowed; he had been wounded at the Somme 37 years earlier. A back row of young people wondered whether church attitudes would change: they had been denied group walks in the woods up the dale after Sunday evensong. The curator of the Bowes Museum, a vast Anglo-French institution opposite the vicarage, could not forget the major financial problems of his museum.

Under his bushy eyebrows the Bishop gazed round as if worried by the conventional passivity he saw as a sickness of the Church of England. He would quote F. D. Maurice: 'We have been dosing our people with religion, when what they want is not that but the living

God.' Ramsey challenged the church to take risks and not sink into depressive introversion. A majority of the Church of England and the Methodist Church were willing years later to take the risk of reunion in his unity plan but were defeated by a minority of over-cautious clerics. The Archbishop again used a medical metaphor and said he felt 'wounded'. Cure of souls in the mid-twentieth century urgently required the churches to change if they were to live in the minds and hearts of the new generation.

A hundred years earlier the scene at Barnard Castle had been even more daunting. Burials in the church stank and graves in the churchyard polluted the houses down the bank to the river Tees below the church. The town suffered a major epidemic of Asiatic cholera. In Sunderland and other north-eastern industrial districts this disease came in through the ports and spread rapidly in homes without drains, piped water or adequate ventilation. Animal manure and carcasses piled up in the dark narrow yards when butchers threw out their offal. Open cesspits, tanning processing pits using human urine, uninspected slaughterhouses and a factory processing guano and fish added to the stench and filthy living conditions. Teenage cohabitation, annual babies and no public relief led to poverty and sometimes robbery. A judge at Durham stigmatized Barnard Castle as 'a sink of vice and profligacy'. Nearly 200 died in the epidemics and there were 1,300 cases of premonitory diarrhoea. The majority of the town's population were sick.

There were two heroes of these dark days – William Ranger the sanitary inspector and George Dugard the vicar. The inspector's report secured a new water supply, drainage system and the clearing out of unhealthy refuse from the houses. George Dugard had been systematic and courageous in visiting those suffering from Asiatic cholera, and it meant much to Barnard Castle people that he was alongside them in the epidemic. He contributed to the inspector's report and topped the poll for the new Local Board of Health.

Burials ceased in the church and a new cemetery replaced the disastrously sited old churchyard. Dugard worked with other religious communities, Free Church and Roman Catholic, and the population was enabled to experience more healthy living conditions in this isolated town.

Townspeople in the next century naturally interpreted 'cure of souls' as being committed to the welfare of the community. In the 1950s the church acquired a younger staff, some with young families. Babies were born in the vicarage again. Colleagues arrived who had skills and enthusiasms which the community needed: Frank Wright, an ex-RAF POW, later Canon of Manchester, and also a Granada TV presenter of religious programmes; Roger Gaunt, the founder of the St Endellion Music Festival who did much for the town's music; Alan Pyburn, a former Cambridge college chaplain, a wit and artist and Philip Wright, an able scientist who also taught at Barnard Castle School.

Frank Wright's farewell sermon at a crowded evensong in 1955 hinted at the philosophy which lay behind ministry, the conviction that to share in worship could nurture imagination and transfigure life. He described the small East German town of Mühlberg which lay just beyond the perimeter barbed wire of the camp where he had been a prisoner. The prisoners could see the townsfolk going about their lives apparently oblivious of the thousands of men from all over Europe incarcerated alongside them. His unstated moral was the temptation, whether in north-country towns or anywhere on planet Earth, for humankind to live in indifference to its neighbours. Imagination fatigue is a sickness of the soul.

Hundreds in Teesdale worked at the Glaxo factory, as scientific process workers in the pharmaceutical industry producing penicillin. How was the work of the town to be represented in worship? The mysterious relationships of cure of souls were symbolized in a tele-vised harvest festival in 1955. A young church member who worked at Glaxo presented a phial of penicillin which was laid on the altar. She was followed by a Durham Light Infantry soldier (a battalion was in camp in the parish) who presented one of its historic silver bugles, while a young farmer offered a sheaf from his harvest and a café proprietor symbols of his tourist work. All four were young men and women: pre-recorded clips of their work were shown in the TV service to viewers. Cure of souls involved working with those making major life decisions, with people who were learning their work, looking forward to marriage and finding somewhere to live, or learning to live alone or with disability.

The imaginative planning and rehearsals for this Sunday evening national television service felt like a twentieth-century sacrament. George Dugard, the vicar one hundred years before, had spoken of the 'utter indifference and apathy to religion of those condemned to live in polluted dwellings'. Now the whole town and millions outside Teesdale could share in their own homes the worship in the church – a thanksgiving for new life.

The popular artist Giles made a notable addition to that Sunday service. His cartoon, soon up in every pub in the town, fastened on the fact that this was the last BBC harvest festival before advertising came on the screens with the birth of ITV the following Sunday. He drew the interior of the church with a shopkeeper advertising his wares on a poster, the organist thumping a riotous choirboy and the vicar in the pulpit denouncing Mammon.

Even in the fifties there seemed to be an over-abundance of meetings. But they did sometimes have results: a redeveloped nursing home, a new house for a headmaster. Some meetings with young people led to group weekends at St John's in the Vale, Helvellyn, and to drama and music sometimes augmenting evening worship. Then there was much planning over the legalities and the ceremony, to be presided over by the Queen Mother, of the handing over of the trusteeship of the Bowes Museum to Durham County Council. Perhaps more important for the cure of souls were the hours of meetings that went into the demolition of the old dark-green-and-cream-painted Institute, a construction of astonishing gloom and inconvenience, and the building of a modern hall with a fine contemporary mural by a Teesdale artist, Douglas Pittuck.

Of course in Teesdale there was always the chance of storm and snow. The surpliced choir on a Rogation Day procession were marooned in a barn up the dale to escape a blizzard in May. Our MP, Dr Hugh Dalton, evading a downpour on the great field of the Demesnes by the Tees, unexpectedly came to be sheltered with 100 followers in the Vicarage. Could we give them all tea? Yes. Cake? No. 'Don't ask for cake,' said one firm mother from a Durham mining family to her hungry son. 'Don't you know you are in a vicarage?' Laughter, hopes to change life, the outstanding beauty of the fauna and flora of the dale, especially *gentiana verna* and *primula farinosa* with the lapwings calling overhead in early summer, contributed to nature's hidden cure of souls.

The Durham Light Infantry bugle and the film clip of a platoon exercising up the dale hinted at the friendly relationships between the church and the battalions stationed in the camps around the town. When the Gloucestershire Regiment came back from the Korean War the padre, S. J. Davies, who had been a POW for two and a half years in Chinese hands with 400 men from the regiment after the Battle of the Imjin River, preached movingly about their efforts to protect the city of Seoul and their experience of captivity.

Regiments might provide Sunday School teachers; one teacher brought a stone he had picked up the previous Wednesday in a North African desert exercise to make his lesson more vivid. The church shared the army families' joys and sorrows – the 12-year-old who was the most dashing of the winter tobogganists died of untreatable leukaemia. He was at the centre of many prayers. Church people were on the station platform when the troops departed in the middle of the night for the ill-judged Suez expedition. The fifties were hard for the services as they saw the end of the Empire. They needed open homes, a warm-hearted welcome, a willingness to argue and a church which encouraged them when they returned to England, uncertain of their next posting or job.

The church had a flourishing Guild for adolescents providing a much needed social amenity. Their increasing affection for the church and their understanding of its role in the community contrasted with the current comment that worship is 'boring, boring, boring'. Cure of souls meant encouraging imaginative activities.

Reflecting 50 years after leaving Barnard Castle, I realize that it's no longer possible, or perhaps even desirable, to visit every home in a parish. But the church will have a caring and creative role in the community. Worship of many varieties with drama, poetry, music and dance will celebrate with freshly imagined words the themes of Christmas, Good Friday, Easter and the spirit-led community. The loving care, the cure of souls and bodies will continue to be at the core of the Christian hope.

Mallerstang

While George Dugard was struggling with Asiatic cholera, over the Pennines another priest, Joseph Brunskill, was sent to the hamlet of Mallerstang as curate (1853–57). Mallerstang Dale is remote, hidden, guarded by the ruins of Pendragon Castle, restored in the seventeenth century by Lady Ann Clifford but de-roofed by her son who had no interest in such an out-of-the-way home. The parson before Brunskill had been suspended for intemperance, no doubt due to the loneliness of the nine years he had spent in this tiny Westmorland group of farms on the little-used road between Kirkby Stephen and Hawes. Fortunately Joseph Brunskill was an energetic 29, the son of a small farmer, a keen teacher of village boys and girls, and with an expertise in the shoeing of horses. The lay people of his previous curacy, the hamlet of Mansergh, had presented him with a 'Memorial' which revealed what 'cure of souls' meant in rural Westmorland. They thanked him for the kind manner in which he had 'instructed the young, visited the sick, and encouraged the aged in the right path towards a happy end'. They tactfully did not mention that he had quarrelled with the squire who had erected an over-large private pew and that his high church habit of giving communion to the dying did not please bishops with narrow views. As his biographer John Breay put it, 'Brunskill was his own Bishop!'

The system of the Established Church might have been designed to depress country clergy. They were paid very little and if non-graduates they had no hope of 'promotion'. The bishop in the diocese of Carlisle lived in Rose Castle, a medieval mansion, and was a Prebendary of St Paul's, a member of the House of Lords and Chancellor of another diocese, all of which of course took him away from his own diocese. Theological prejudice sometimes separated him from his clergy. The bishops' conception of the cure of souls of their clergy was often legalistic and impersonal without the happiness of friendship. Country clergy were kept at the bottom.

At Mallerstang and the other fellside parishes Brunskill served, and indeed until his death in 1903 he was controversially outspoken in standing up for the poor. In letters to the press he criticized the Penrith magistrates who imprisoned wanderers from Scotland seeking work.

As a young apprentice to a Sunderland chemist he had seen the poverty, unemployment and hardships of those driven into factory work as children. He read and treasured *The Fleet Papers* by Richard Oastler, the so-called 'King of the Factory Children'. Oastler was imprisoned in the Fleet in London but wrote weekly Papers which pilloried the visiting magistrate in Carlisle Castle, who not only confiscated a debtor's meal but censoriously forbade another prisoner to play the flute.

Though Brunskill was such a battler he believed that cure of souls should be a happy task for a parson with a happy family life. Wherever he went, music and games and love of horses went with him. From the age of 20 he had enjoyed church prayers and community worship. Perhaps because the church paid him so badly, perhaps because of his love of children, perhaps to escape episcopal oversight, he spent ten years as a successful headmaster of Lowther School and did not inform the bishop. Eventually Lord Lowther saw his worth and appointed him as vicar, his first freehold, to the parish of Threlkeld. Here he spent his most fulfilling years. He had a jolly social life. He had not retreated into depressed inaction when the bishop had rejected his plea for building a school for the 20 children at Mallerstang who had to make do with a hay loft at the back of the church. He made sure they were better taught even in such a confined space. His diary often hints at the cost of his cure of souls in remote dales. His diary reads: 'Nov. 22 1853. Received my half years stipend £40.0.0. A good covering of snow fell today.'

Cure of souls in the diocese of Carlisle for the fellside clergy was a hard task. The snow at Mallerstang might be five feet deep and there was little encouragement from tiny congregations. In those fellside parishes cure of souls meant that the parson must be everybody's friend and nobody's enemy. He made sure that children were educated before parents and farmers wanted them in the fields. It meant funding cricket teams, importing lacrosse sticks from Canada and keeping the isolated in touch with the outside world. Reading the papers free in public houses and spreading the news, as well as preaching that duty to one's country was a reasonable requirement even in remote villages, was all related to cure of souls in the eyes of the Fellside parsons.

In 1869, after Brunskill had left, the peace of Mallerstang was disturbed by the construction of the Settle–Carlisle railway, one of the last great manpower engineering works. The muscle of nearly 5,000 navvies was needed. Conditions were primitive and many died in accidents in the sodden and rocky terrain. Horses sank in bogs of sphagnum moss and lost their shoes. The hut camps for the women and children who came with the men were crude and insanitary. The parish register recording infant deaths in the camps makes tragic reading today. Some efforts were made by the churches to provide huts for social life and worship but Mallerstang often tried to keep itself to itself. Long afterwards an Appleby business man recalled a relative saying, 'Don't talk to me about the railway, I was 16 years old when they started to build the line and my father kept me locked away for six years until the men moved on. That's why I never got wed.'

Warcop and Shepreth

Joseph Brunskill's biographer, John Breay, was born at Mallerstang in 1919. He was ordained, the fifth in line in his family to serve as parish priest in the church. Despite a harshly unhappy childhood, disinherited while a Cambridge undergraduate, he became one of the most talented of twentieth-century clergy in rural parishes near Carlisle and later south of Cambridge. He was single and deeply sensitive to the spiritual value of pastoral care and church buildings to small communities. He valued children and saw them as 'children of God' at birth. Baptism was the sacrament which recognized this. He was close to his parishioners whether it was a village headmaster, a shy squire or a farm worker down on his luck. He befriended gypsies, cleaned out blocked downspouts and was remembered sitting at his typewriter, as someone said, like an outraged bustard, protesting at some action of the Church Commissioners (who infuriated him by losing £800,000,000 in unwise speculations). Dr Williams, the philosopher Bishop of Carlisle, who ordained him, won his respect. Theological students at Lincoln visiting Taizé found him a fun companion, deeply committed to faith, prayer and ecumenism. Breay was erudite, humorous, a keen organist, a skilled gardener and an alert naturalist. Occasionally he surprised and delighted churchgoers with his 'Omnibus Prayer' on the lines of 'Let us pray for farmers with foot and mouth and the parish next door about to have a new vicar'.

Cure of souls to this reticent man led him to the marginalized. His historical concerns were with those who suffered from overbearing landlords. His *Light in the Dales: Studies in Religious Dissent and Land Tenure* (1996) traced the sufferings of Roman Catholics, Calvinists, Quakers and (under the Commonwealth) Anglicans. He researched the land tenure consequences for those who suffered as religious minorities whether in the Pilgrimage of Grace standing for the Old Faith or as Levellers preaching English religious freedom.

At his funeral in March 1996 at Shepreth Church, Cambridgeshire, which he had served for 18 years, this shy man asked for a letter to be read to his many friends. His letter, read by a churchwarden, told the ups and downs of ministry, asking for forgiveness where he had hurt anyone or done wrong. He thanked 'those who have given me new insights into the ways of God . . . there have been many moments of pure gold here . . . All through my life there has been this sense of the Presence of Christ among us.' His cure of souls was hidden, private, unobtrusive and his funeral like a dialogue about questioning faith.

His imaginative understanding and magnetic attraction seemed to hint at the hidden God relating to human life, where the dark could be transformed. Breay had been so creative in detail: restoring the woodwork of a country church door, deciphering texts and wills, reorganizing ancient parish charities, caring for his garden and his bees as well as preparing his sermons, sacraments and services so that it was easier to detect the Divine at work in providence and prayer. He was obstinately faithful and was prepared to devote his life to cure of souls, for better for worse, in sickness and in health, and again and again in joy and humour. In his parishes he was simply there, for everyone.

St Peter's, Hale

In the twentieth century the state, urged on by the conscience of the community and political pressures, became increasingly responsible for education, medical care and social welfare. The Church's own structure was partially reformed and the pluralism and the isolation of the poorest and unbeneficed clergy were reduced. Bishops were more pastorally minded, ceased to be absentees and became less authoritarian. In the new and relatively wealthy suburbs such as Hale in Cheshire, Brunskill's eldest son John was first a curate and then vicar. He built St Peter's church and vicarage and visited the new houses as they were occupied. An organized, churchgoing community was created; perhaps there was a tendency for the cure of souls to be seen in terms of churchgoing. But the priest was still there to evoke imaginative and creative forms of thought and life.

As institutions the churches became smaller, especially during and after World War I. Some parishioners did not want deep friendships or family spirit; some wanted to keep themselves to themselves and preserve their own status. But when Brunskill left after a period of illness they described his cure of souls in these words (no doubt over-eulogistic):

The worshippers at St Peter's Church, Hale, desire to place upon record their high appreciation of the services you have rendered during the THIRTY-TWO YEARS you have been with them as Curate in Charge and Vicar of the parish.

During that time you have endeared yourself to all your Parishioners by your inspiring leadership, personal sacrifice and unfailing courtesy, in all your work for the advancement of the Kingdom of God.

As a token of our deep affection they ask your acceptance of this Address with their earnest prayers that the Blessing of Almighty God will continually rest upon your labours and that you may long be spared to continue in your new sphere the work you so dearly love.

Hale, January 1925

Wrenbury

Cure of souls developed as society itself developed. I experienced these changes as a boy in Wrenbury where I was born, a village of about 2,000 people set in the south Cheshire plain, flat and bosky with large dairy farms, in early summer white with damson blossom in all the hedges. My mother was the youngest daughter of Joseph Brunskill, my father the son of a north-country lawyer at St Bees in Cumberland – by an odd coincidence the place where Brunskill had received his meagre training for ordination. My father spent his last 20 years as vicar in this small village. He had been a friend of Dr B. H. Streeter, one of the modern New Testament scholars who accepted Darwin's theory of evolution and believed that J. G. Frazer's *Golden Bough* had much to teach the Church. As a teenager Darwin and Marx became important for me – Freud had to wait. My father believed that there was not sufficient historical evidence to decide without doubt on the historicity of the Virgin Birth – not because of the impossibility of miracles but because 'maybe it was the will of God that we should not know how his Son was born. God may consider that such knowledge is irrelevant to our salvation'. There was always a microscope in his study. He worked on the *Patristic Greek Lexicon* eventually edited by Dr Geoffrey Lampe and read current theology as well as growing rare alpines. Interested young people were often in the house and at the piano.

Cure of souls involved deep and sensitive personal relationships. The cure was not administrative or organizational but evoked human friendship. As in earlier centuries those on the margin were known and appreciated. We cycled out one evening every Christmas to the gypsy huts on the heath, creeping into their homes on hands and knees, bringing with us mince pies and presents. On Sundays the kitchen always smelt of beer because an old cobbler shared the dinner that day. Disaster struck a young man slaking lime in a milk churn. His employer neither supervised nor insured him. The lime flew up in his face and destroyed his eyes. My father and the leading Methodist layman went round the village collecting enough to have him retrained, given a weekly allowance and a repair shop for shoes. There were protests from the vicarage to the powers that be: inadequate rural housing, no piped water, electricity or drainage system. At my father's funeral someone wrote, 'Thank God, parson was for the workers'. Someone else said: 'Fancy wasting so many years in a small village,' but the village disagreed.

The church worked for minorities. In the tuberculosis sanatorium there was a Jewish patient. My father, who was fluent in Hebrew, asked whether he might read the psalms to him in Hebrew when he came on his regular visit and the patient said: 'Please do'. My father also read the psalms alone in Hebrew at the daily morning services in church when the bell was rung. No one else was there except, some said, 'the angels'.

When foot and mouth disease devastated the dairy herds both farmers and farm labourers suffered severely. From my bedroom window I could see huge coal fires incinerating the cattle burnt day and night, and the smell of burning flesh drifted over the fields. It mattered that there was a family from the vicarage to go round the farms and share the grimness. And as in those days, most women gave up their profession on marrying, my mother, like many vicars' wives, found a creative outlet for her skills and her pleasure in life.

The cure of souls for over a century had included relevant, imaginative and learned preaching. My father's last sermon exactly a month before he died on 7 September 1935 ended with these words:

Man's life may not be long but it is a most serious affair. It does matter whether we dedicate our lives to the service of God or not. There are Germans who thank God that they are not Jews, and Italians who praise Him because they are not Abyssinian. It is high time that men should stop sneering at other races. There is anxiety over the face of the whole globe. Men wonder what is coming. They dread the uprising of nations and the antagonisms of colour. No one can tell what in 50 years' time will be the state of the world. The one hope of mankind is Jesus Christ with his peaceable wisdom which overcomes the evil of the world. He alone is not superficial and can lead men to look where true riches are to be found and crown the faithful with eternal life.
(Extract from sermon on 7 August 1935)

A number of those who heard the sermon did not return from World War II, including one who always sat beside me in the choir.

Sheffield

'Receive the cure of souls which is mine and thine' is the phrase used by the bishop to designate a shared ministry. The bishop's especial task is to share a prophetic vision of God's will for humanity and to find women and men to serve in the ministry of the parishes. The three parishes where I was invited to serve in 1942, Barrow-in-Furness, Sunderland and Attercliffe in Sheffield, were all industrial areas with sparsely attended churches. All three parishes had been bombed in the previous six months. At Attercliffe the Waterloo church had been destroyed but the vicarage had survived and after repairs, at which we all worked, became the home of a team of eight men and women, two of whom were Jewish Christian refugees from the Nazis.

A component of the Spitfire RAF fighter was manufactured in one of the parish's steel foundries so the Nazi raids continued. In the hills above Sheffield a rapidly expanding prisoner of war camp was established and some of the architect prisoners were escorted down to the Don valley to redraw plans for the new community church centres which it was hoped would replace the blitzed buildings. Today many of the parishioners are Muslim, and the German plans which included a beer hall by the church were exhibited in the city library but never built. The church where I first celebrated Holy Communion is now used by a non-Christian group.

It was Bishop Leslie Hunter's dynamic cure of souls which had drawn so many priests to Sheffield. From youth he knew the European churches and with Bishop Bell of Chichester visited Germany and found ways to rescue a few of the Jews. He admired the Scandinavian churches and their prophets, especially Kai Munk, the Danish priest martyr. In the House of Lords Hunter was often an unpopular prophet. When the war ended he pleaded for the early return of prisoners of war. He enabled the German POWs at the Lodge Moor camp to have a Christmas service in Sheffield Cathedral. He joined in setting up the ecumenical relief bodies which developed into Christian Aid. He shared the determined tolerance of Sheffield east-enders who welcomed our German Jewish team member when she went shopping even though she then had little English and the German raids on Yorkshire continued.

Hunter had a vision of a cure of souls which challenged a world scarred by war and a church still not ecumenical or reformed. He admired Baron von Hügel, the Roman Catholic modernist and mystic. He advocated fundamental change both in society and the Church and believed that the intelligence of the people he had served in Tyneside, London and South Yorkshire deserved much more creative and risk-taking leadership. He was a disciple of William Temple and felt that his early death was a blow to all the churches. Hunter was honest, gritty, often unpopular and prepared to face the deep causes of the alienation of modern society from the gospel. He was also complex; a delight playing Mozart at his piano but dark when depressed. He valued silence, sensing that words cannot articulate the perplexities and tragedies of life. He seemed to answer my search for a strategist for the spirit in the cure of souls and I chose his diocese to begin work in 1942.

The gap between the church and the workers was wide. The bishop brought in clergy and women who would devote themselves to bridging that gap. New residential training centres at Whirlow and Hollowford were founded and staffed so that apprentices and parish members could think and together become more articulate. Hunter invited many clergy couples to move to Sheffield to challenge the shut-in world of conventional religion; they included Oliver and Ursula Tomkins, Noel and Ruth Wardle-Harpur and Alan and Delia Ecclestone. The Ecclestones stayed 27 years in the east end parish of Darnall. For Alan Ecclestone, artists, authors and poets were God's spies and the catholicity of his mind is revealed in his own books, especially *Yes to God*, *The Night Sky of the Lord* and *Gather the Fragments*.

Hunter also kept in touch with the priest-worker movement in the Roman Catholic Church in France and grieved when it was suppressed partly because of right-wing influence. Hunter brought ecumenical brothers from Taizé to stay in Attercliffe, and the creative missioner Ted Wickham, with his wife Helen, to head the Sheffield Industrial Mission (afterwards frowned on by a more narrowly orientated bishop). Hunter's style led him to listen to the steel workers, sitting among them while the metal was 'cooking'. This personally-led, non-judgemental sharing approach was new, as was the fact that Hunter quietly but critically supported the Labour Party. The souls for whom he cared were often those of Sheffield people who would say: 'The church is not for the likes of us.' Cure of souls required the appreciation of those who had inherited a secular mind-set. It was not a case of personal alienation: the industrial cities of Europe had always been outside the churches. Charles Péguy had noticed before World War I that 'the Curés had lost the parishes'.

Hunter interpreted cure of souls in a community sense; souls wither or grow much influenced by the culture of the day. The Church existed for the nations and their communities and not for self-promotion. Its task was more like that of a midwife than an authoritarian father figure. Cure of souls in Hunter's eyes meant living the life the world needs if the earth is not to destroy itself. When the atom bombs were exploded in Japanese cities there was a church-inspired move of protest in Sheffield's east end. Hunter said in public that the excuses for destroying so many thousands of Japanese lives were 'humbug'. Cure of souls meant encouraging a willingness to carry personal responsibility without which the welfare state would be just so much idealistic legislation and would fail. Tough, hard work needed to be voluntarily done in the youth clubs and summer camps, as well as in the social services, the schools and the national health service. Cure of the souls of the defeated nations also mattered. To quote Hunter writing to his diocese, 'If Germany is not to become a festering sore in Europe, its people must be given something to hope for.'

After his death the European Bursary Trust, which he had founded, used his estate to enable one or two members of the church, year after year, to live abroad. Still being in their twenties they became well acquainted with the society and church of the country where they were living – Finland, France, Italy, East and West Germany. From 1983 to 1993 grants were made to take groups of young people from English parishes to Taizé and in 1986 helped finance the London Taizé meeting when 25,000 young people from Europe came to think and worship together in London.

The cure of souls in tiny fellside hamlets, small towns, midland villages and the east end communities of great industrial cities, in Cumbria, Durham, Cheshire and South Yorkshire, is typical of thousands of parishes not only in Britain but in Europe. Many of those who do not worship regularly wish to give thanks for a birth, to mark a wedding and to celebrate the end of a life. Christian communities inherit a spiritual tradition of sacraments and shared thinking through Bible reading, and a mutual concern for each other both in times of stress and of happiness.

Hunter used to tell this parable with eastern origins to suggest that we should not easily assume that everything will get better and better and that inevitable progress is part of the divine plan. The parable goes to the heart of the mutual relationship described as cure of souls.

As the threats of war and the cries of the dispossessed were sounding in his ears, Western Man fell into an uneasy sleep. In his sleep he dreamed that he entered the spacious store in which the gifts of God to men are kept, and addressed the angel behind the counter, saying: 'I have run out of the fruits of the Spirit. Can you restock me?' When the angel seemed about to say no, he burst out 'In place of war, afflictions, injustice, lying and lust, I need love, joy, peace, integrity, discipline. Without these I shall be lost.' And the angel behind the counter replied, 'We do not stock fruits, only seeds.'

(Leslie Hunter, *The Seed and the Fruit*, p. 12)

Let that outspoken Anglican layman, Samuel Johnson, give a verdict on all these endeavours. 'Sir, the life of a parson, of a conscientious clergyman, is not easy. I have always considered a clergyman as the father of a larger family than he is able to maintain. I would rather have Chancery suits upon me than the cure of souls.' It is not easy but it is a calling. It is a willingness to search for meaning, to look for the finger of God in everyday and sometimes boring events. To give particular prayer and thought and particular kindness to all members of the human family constitutes cure of souls. It is to imagine and work for a Kingdom of God, a brave new world, in every community large and small.

References

Barbour, Robin S. of Fincastle, private correspondence.

Breay, John, *A Fellside Parson: Joseph Brunskill and his Diaries, 1826–1903*. Norwich, Canterbury Press, 1995.

Breay, John, *Light in the Dales*. Norwich, Canterbury Press, 1996.

Ecclestone, Alan, *Gather the Fragments*. Sheffield, Cairns, 1993.

Ecclestone, Alan, *The Night Sky of the Lord*. London, Darton, Longman & Todd, 1980.

Ecclestone, Alan, *Yes to God*. London, Darton, Longman & Todd, 1975.

Gorringe, Tim, *Alan Ecclestone: Priest as Revolutionary*. Sheffield, Cairns, 1994.

Hamilton, John, *Mallerstang Dale: the Head of Eden*. Cotham, Broadcast, 1993.

Hewitt, Gordon, ed., *Strategist for the Spirit: Leslie Hunter, Bishop of Sheffield 1939–62*. Oxford, Becket, 1985.

Hunter, Leslie, *The Seed and the Fruit*. London, SCM Press, 1953.

Keily, Pamela, *Memoirs: Haphazard Recollections of a Lifetime of Religious Drama*. Otley, Smith Settle, 1986.

Latham, F. A., *Wrenbury and Marbury: the History of Two Parishes and the Nearby Villages*. Wrenbury, The Local History Group, 1999.

Mitchell, W. R. and Joy, David, *Settle–Carlisle Railway*. Clapham, N. Yorkshire, Dalesman, 1979.

Ramsey, Michael, *The Christian Priest Today*. London, SPCK, 1985.

Webster, Alan, *Broken Bones May Joy*. London, SCM Press, 1968.

Wickham, E. R., *Church and People in an Industrial City*. London, Lutterworth, 1957.

Wilkinson, Alan, *Barnard Castle, Historic Market Town*. Otley, Smith Settle, 1998.

Wright, Frank, *Pastoral Care Revisited*. London, SCM Press, 1996.

2 VILLAGE AND CITY:
Bright Lights from Small Flames

O God, make the door of this Church wide enough
to receive all who need human love and fellowship;
narrow enough to shut out all envy, pride and strife.
Make its threshold smooth enough to be no stumbling
block to children, nor to straying feet,
but rugged and strong to turn back the tempter's power.
O God, make the doorway of this Church
an entrance to your eternal kingdom. Amen.

(Prayer used at Barnham Broom Church in thanksgiving for its
restoration, May 2000; a prayer written by Bishop Thomas Ken for
St Stephen's, Walbrook, a Wren church beside Mansion House, now
the home of a Henry Moore altar and the headquarters of the
Samaritans)

As the institutional churches in Europe decline numerically it is
surprising that despite a shortage of cash there are signs of hope and
many fresh initiatives. This chapter looks at four examples from
urban and rural England. In each area the church communities are
small – around 100 in the city parish, a dozen or so in many of the
villages – but all are working for an alert and friendly future where
loving service for each other and informed prayer for humanity are
realities.

Barnham Broom

The 13 rural Norfolk parishes known as Barnham Broom and Upper
Yare, with a population of about 3,000, are accustomed to the difficulties of keeping the church alive. In the past they have suffered
from the absenteeism of bishops and vicars. There are tales of

archdeacons descending on negligent villages and ordering them to rebuild their towers. They are resilient and independent and when suggestions come from Norwich that they should have weekly services in each one of their churches, they wonder who will heat and clean these, especially the churches with bats. In the smaller villages with less than a hundred inhabitants the normal congregations of eight or ten become 40, 60, 80 or even 115 at Christmas. Then the congregations can occasionally be larger than the population of the hamlets as relatives flock in.

Sometimes the churches are the only stimulus for village events, and can be full for weddings and funerals. If there is a service for the whole group on the first Sunday in the month, the coffee reception in a farmhouse is long, leisurely and exceedingly well informed. The group service is fresh and enterprising, a major source of group fellowship. In spite of this, some never come out of their own villages whatever happens.

In the large villages the community is more fractured and more fluid. There can be a number of primary school parents, and a Sunday School and a family service flourish. Then the kids go to secondary school and vanish from church and sometimes the parents move. Task-orientated groups, ringers at one church, choir at another, social groups at others, help to keep the children in touch. Many of the younger generation find the clergy fun, but buildings without heating, loos or kitchens discourage them.

The spirit of the group is impressive, with small cores of people who take responsibility with the minister, or without the minister if he or she is ill. The Rector of Barnham Broom, Canon Cathy Milford, inherited and developed a Group Ministry Team and Group Council. The ministry team of about nine members resources the worship, thinking and planning all in a pastoral context, thinking of the needs of many different individuals and committed to listening and making connections. The Rector's width of experience in England and abroad enables her to act as a filter of central church burdens: 'some of the legislation is potty' is her shrewd verdict. The Ordained Local Ministers (unpaid) need the support of a well-informed monthly group meeting with Holy Communion or Compline. Bible study and contemplation are experienced in the group programme.

Developments in theology and spiritual life are studied and discussed in unhurried sessions, where the varieties and individual understandings of faith can be shared. It's hard work but creative and imaginative.

Through discussion, plans for action bubble up. The varieties of opinion can be fruitful. Thought for the children is especially important. Teachers at a village church school, Anglican, Baptist and a Plymouth Brother, with the Rector, began a Friday afternoon voluntary club when school was over. The club has 30 on the books, one-third of the children in the school. Its weekly programme includes games, crafts, the telling of Bible and religious stories, and snacks. Memorized verses of the Bible are used as passwords next week! There is a feeling about the church and the school, because both are sensed to belong to the village, which encourages support. Those who maintain the Friday Club find it demanding at the end of the school week, but as one of them said, 'It's sowing seeds. It's as worthwhile as creating a garden.'

Some churches need serious repairs and English Heritage is underfunded. The diocese is paying less, and in ten years' time the parishes must pay more and get used to paying for the parsons; local landowners in some parishes keep the churches in good order, but some landowners have left and some tenant farmers have lost the tradition of caring for the church, and this shows. But churchwardens find ways of coping and, as the Rector says, 'My money is on there being churches in the countryside for some time to come, Barclays Bank notwithstanding.' They wish the diocese would appeal (like the Norwich Cathedral appeal on its way to £10,000,000), so that each church could be given £5,000 for improvements within the building – heating and other amenities. That would do wonders in the next five years and would recognize how overtiring so many church buildings can be for the ministers and worshippers.

If you visited any of these parishes for a Group Service or a service for a major festival or special occasion, you would be welcomed at the start of the worship by someone from that local host church. The service would be more imaginative than the official service book. If you had young ones with you they would not say 'Boring . . . !' You might even be startled into laughter as well as moved by prayer. One eloquent sermon, drawing on a critical study of the Bible, led to a conclusion urging that after 800 years of Christian worship on that spot the time had come to spend £1,000 and install amenities. Another of these ancient village churches held a Candlemas service; each worshipper was given a light, and slowly in the silence the church was transformed, like a sacrament for the week. The dominant feeling is not depression but admiration: you hear a sermon opening up what God is doing in the global village today. In winter some of these churches can feel like skeletons, but spring comes and with it a resurrection life. The small core group has maintained a place of faith where much can grow.

Binham and Blakeney

The celebration of the Millennium was a challenge to Christian communities worldwide. How best to commemorate the 2000th anniversary of the birth of Christ? Some tiny north Norfolk parishes decided to produce a passion play not only in modern English but so written that the cast could stop acting events of long ago and live the parts today. The vicar, John Penny, and his collaborator, a retired headmaster, Jim Woodhouse, a skilled producer of pageants, wrote the text. The vicar had spent two years on the work. He was inspired by the Bible translation of William Tyndale, who had been barbarously executed in 1536 for his determination that people should be in touch with the Gospels in their own language without the intervention of the church. Penny's play *Jesus in the Mirror* required a cast of over 30 and another 20 to stage it in Blakeney village and in Binham Priory. The four performances drew packed audiences of over 200 each night and everyone was deeply impressed. It was local and not widely advertised.

The aim, in contrast to Oberammergau or many British productions of medieval mystery plays, was to re-imagine the Gospels in the idiom of contemporary north Norfolk life. The language and the attitudes were contemporary. The Governor attacked the 'chief cleric' who was demanding Jesus' execution. 'You religious creep. You make me sick. I wash my hands of the whole business.' The lifestyle was contemporary. So the marriage of Cana was imagined in

London where the off-licence failed and the wine was inadequate. The motives for the Lord's 'miracle' were in part to save the bride's mother from a heart attack, in part to show that Jesus was not to be called 'Misery Guts' like John the Baptist. It became more than a play for the talented men, women and children of those villages. The Spirit was present with a special freshness, the symbolic stories came to life. I remembered Michael Ramsey's saying, 'God is Christlike and in him is nothing un-Christlike at all'.

Sheffield

In 1998 the Anglicans and Methodists in a Sheffield parish founded a Local Ecumenical Project with united worship, a common purse and shared ownership of property, including the valuable site of the Victorian parish church (built to seat 700) which had been demolished because it was judged unsafe by the insurers. Plans were agreed for future developments, including the re-ordering of the Methodist church to make it more convenient. They have their own eucharistic rite for the main Sunday morning service, more flexible than either the Anglican or Methodist tradition. On Sundays at 8 a.m. there is Holy Communion according to the Book of Common Prayer and in the afternoon/evening Anglican or Methodist orders of service. Competition is over: instead there is a feeling of delight at being able to learn gradually to share each other's worship with a weekly united congregation of 100–120.

Within the parish, whose population is about 8,000, are many other churches and institutions. Among them are the King's Centre, a 400-strong free evangelical gathered charismatic church, a large new Sheffield Citadel being built by the Salvation Army, Quakers meeting within the Anglican/Methodist premises, a small synagogue, a Tibetan Buddhist centre and many principled humanists and agnostics. The vicar, Nicholas Jowett, believes that what is needed is a modest exploratory theology. Care is taken to keep up to date with modern theological thinking; among those theologians whose works have been helpful are Bishop David Jenkins, formerly of Durham, Professor John Rogerson of Sheffield, Canon Tom Wright of Westminster Abbey and Robert Funk of The Jesus Seminar.

I mentioned to the vicar that the practice and thinking of this group reminded me of Charles Darwin's enthusiasm for the work of worms in creating a fertile soil which grows the wheat and the other crops. Darwin admired the worms' resolute but unpretentious work in fertilizing the ground, a work unseen yet crucial in the complex task of producing the humus essential to fertility. In reply Nicholas Jowett mentioned the contemporary scientist Stephen Jay Gould who has worked on bacteria, which in Jowett's words are 'incredibly more tough and long lived than humanity... Jesus Christ's image of yeast in a huge amount of dough is a powerful one. The kingdom of God is like bacteria.'

The author of *God of Surprises*, Fr Gerard Hughes SJ, made a major contribution to the spirituality of this congregation with his seminars and his ability to convey the unfussy normalness of the practice of the hidden presence of God. Because the community itself works at its own liturgies for special occasions it is aware of the variety of religious experience. Symbols, silence, poetry and colour, light and darkness, movement and drama all have their place. Different and diverse religious backgrounds are respected by guarding against the over-use of divine names. Of course, as anyone who has done this will know, the creation of new services is time-consuming.

The resurrection of this religious community in Sheffield required tough decisions combined with patience over the years. It might have failed. If they had not been realistic the church would have fossilized. The heritage societies might have insisted that the congregation should devote its energies to that impressive 1869 Victorian edifice even though they acknowledged that the foundations were inadequate. The Methodist authorities might have decided to sell their valuable premises and not join in such a risky liaison with an Anglican church. The bishop and the archdeacon might have hesitated and said 'Better not'. The older members of both churches might have refused to adapt to the crisis. A few did pull out. But the clergy listened to those concerned and did not try to rush the fraught congregations. There was willing acceptance of ecumenism. It was a triumph of grass roots discipleship greatly to the credit of Sheffield.

Time alone will tell whether St Andrew's Anglican Methodist

Church will grow so that it has the kind of power shown by the 400-strong King's Centre, which adopts the Pentecostal variety of Christianity. Some, according to the vicar, hope for well imagined, freshly minted worship. Some hope for more 'exploratory theology that allows historical questions into the central events of our faith . . . We can train, trust and talk to each other in so many ways; top-down control really denies the Holy Spirit . . . Faith is not knowledge and we must gladly live with the many things we cannot know for certain . . . Some wonder whether we might be a more attractive church if we just were quietly getting on with a way of life which you talk about only when asked to. My vision is for a truly ecumenical meeting point for worship, study and creative events, a community in which many people can find support for their personal spiritual journey.'

Two new lively communities have recently grown up in this area of Sheffield. In 1997 the Lincoln Theological Institute for the Study of Religion and Society was opened, attached to Sheffield University. It has researched many subjects: health care, hospital chaplaincy, the work of women priests and statistics for church growth and decline. The Director, Dr Martyn Percy, edits the quarterly magazine *Modern Believing*. The Institute's library, lectures and staff are of value to the parishes.

Close by at the old church of St Mary's, Bramall Lane, more than two and a half million pounds has been spent to convert the building for many community uses. At its centre is a small church. Sheffield City Council and other public bodies, including European regenerating funds, have given their support for 'St Mary 2000', which re-equipped one of Sheffield's landmarks, not far from the station and the United football ground, daily passed by many thousands on the new inner ring road. It had been built by Parliamentary grant in 1830, rendered unusable by the 1940 Blitz and, after long indecision, rebuilt as a church and community centre with halls for different activities in 1957 under the wise leadership of Canon Stephen Burnett.

Before the Millennium the vicar, Julian Sullivan, and his assistant, Dr Michael Bayley, with a small, highly committed group and the tiny, fiercely loyal Anglican congregation of about 30, began replanning for the next century. Encouraged by grants from the Church Urban Fund they set out to raise nearly three million pounds. They ensured that a church presence remained in the inner city area and that the church continued to make a contribution to the social, economic and spiritual welfare of the area – one of the hundred most disadvantaged wards in the whole country. Now the church can continue to provide the highly valued training centre for people with learning difficulties as well as other community facilities. The local authorities, other social services and the church have combined in 'St Mary's 2000' to help one of the most deprived inner city areas.

Dickleburgh and the Pulhams, Norfolk

Finding a vicar for these small villages on the Suffolk/Norfolk border is never easy. There are only 3,000 people scattered over a large area divided into six parishes. The responsibility to appoint is shared by the diocese and the people of the parishes, theoretically involving the Prime Minister and the Lord Chancellor. Recently there was a long vacancy. James, the eight-year-old son of the chairman of one village Council, heard his parents worrying about there being no vicar, and clergy not replying to invitations. 'So,' said James, 'I leapt to the Internet to say we needed a vicar. Janice replied. We now have her. We are all happy.'

Before she trained for ordination, Janice Scott was a physiotherapist at Fakenham in Norfolk. She is an able preacher, teacher and storyteller and her sermons and children's tales on a website are surfed from Singapore to Kansas. She picked up James' plea for a vicar, applied to the diocesan authorities and moved from a Norwich suburban parish adjoining the university to the deep country. A former priest in that area who was also gloriously happy described the area as 'the true wilderness'. Nine months after her move this is how Janice Scott talks of her parishes and speculates on their future. I am quoting her letter at length, believing that its details will resonate with many readers.

Things are going well here, although obviously there are always problems in any parish or group of parishes. However, these do seem to be minor and cope-able with so far. One of the under-lying difficulties of the work (as ever) is resistance to change, and this can be particularly awkward if there is a small but steady congregation. They are my friends and I do not wish to lose them. So change has to be introduced very slowly and with good com-munication all along the way.

I've also found all six of the parishes to be somewhat insular. For instance, a central figure in Pulham Market, whom everyone knows and who is at the helm of village life, will be unknown in Dickleburgh just three miles down the road. This does tend to produce hidden barriers, so I find I need to expend a lot of energy in encouraging benefice meetings and get-togethers.

Surprisingly, financial problems are few. Every village has at least one charitable trust, and all these trusts have close connections with the church for historical reasons. The rector of the parish is automatically a member of the trust, so there are unexpected sources of income due to wise investments.

Happily the churches have 'soft walls' – i.e. it's quite difficult to separate church and village. The church very definitely belongs to the village, and is owned by all including those who never darken its doors, but who always support it at village fetes etc. During the summer I sometimes wasn't sure whether the fete was being held by the village or the church, they're so intermingled. And the village tends to turn out en masse for big occasions like Christmas. We had two midnights which each attracted 85 people, plus two crib services, one of which attracted 250 people. Each church had a communion on Christmas Day – around 30 each.

Pulham Market is linked with the Methodists, so almost every-thing is ecumenical. So much so, that people have said: 'There's no difference, I sometimes go to one, sometimes to the other.' There is also a big 'Praise' service once a month which travels around three or four villages and several denominations. This attracts over 100, mostly young people, so as a result, we've offered Pulham Market church as a 'home' to these youngsters, to do as they wish. They've started a service 'NlightN' – enlighten – once a month in which they cater for all age groups, but no sermon. It attracts around 65, even on Boxing Day. I think it will grow, and 50 of those 65 are young, quite a number are children. It's very exciting for me and I hope it will continue.

I have quite a lot of involvement in our two local schools, as a governor of each (again, automatic as rector – they're both church schools) and in assemblies and services in church from time to time. I have also taken assembly at the C of E secondary school, Archbishop Sancroft in Harleston. I've always been warmly welcomed. This veers into the field of social helpfulness, since the school occasionally sends troubled parents in my direction.

We also have copious Beavers, Cubs, Scouts and Brownies who mostly meet in church premises, and one Monday evening 'Sunday School' known as 'Trailblazers'. The only other Sunday School offers Advent and Lent blocks of meeting/teaching – Advent culminating in a crib service, Lent culminating in a Good Friday event for children.

I've made a big effort to support local societies and events, if only in a small way. The Surgery Support Group is thriving and covers all my villages, so I get to that if I can, and have put in an appearance at the Horticultural Society and the British Legion – am chaplain now. Also it is immensely important to support local shops, so I drop in to the shop in each village from time to time. In fact I think one of the most important aspects of my work has been to be seen around. (In the local pub, the landlord has my drink poured out by the time I reach the bar counter! This reflects the time I spend in there . . .) The local councils also work closely with the church and, from time to time, I have had phone calls from councillors asking me to visit needy people.

In ten years' time? Well, it does seem that the day of the massive institution is coming to an end. Many societies – WI, Lions, Rotary, children's uniformed organizations etc. – have much lower membership now than they once had, and this is certainly true in the church. The concept of 'duty' seems to have all but disappeared (thank goodness!) so those who attend come because they want to. Therefore church has to be good and worthwhile and to fill people's needs.

I think the church buildings in these country parishes will

survive, because of the big upsurge in interest in our historical roots. And maybe we should be looking much more in that direction – perhaps we should go all out to present interesting, welcoming, lively tourist attractions which are a pleasure to visit and which tell something of the story of God in a modern, up-market way. And perhaps we should market our churches commercially to attract visitors, since visitors bring money. We'd need excellent facilities such as small café areas and loos, and good shops within each church selling audio tapes, videos, books and rosaries, as well as tourist mementoes. And perhaps tourists should be able to log on to an e-mail list in the church, so that they can receive regular e-mail letters about the church. There would be computer and Internet facilities within each church, so that visitors could take part in a virtual service, or find prayers or music, or find out which churches to visit on this particular tour.

But that's all for tourists. What about the church members? I don't think there will ever come a time when Christians no longer wish to meet together, but I do think that meeting will need to become much more flexible. Already Sunday is a far from ideal day for many families, so I think the main service of worship may need to be at a different time, say early Wednesday evening for instance. Those unable to attend the service, for whatever reason, would be able to share in it via the Internet, for it would be easy to video the service and send it on to the church's web page as it was happening. The housebound would be in regular contact, and would be able to join in the service which would be interactive, so that someone from home could, for instance, lead the prayers.

The church is no longer the main means either of social contact or of entertainment. Those functions are mostly done much better elsewhere (such as in the village shop or community centre), so the church needs to concentrate on its real task – helping people meet with God. While church services and liturgy can aid this process, they can also be a real hindrance for many people, so something needs to be devised which will speak to non-church people in a language they can understand. Again, this may well happen largely through the Internet, where people will be able to meet in much more global groups with others from around the world. I think the local church may find itself concentrating on less frequent but well prepared services and on 'special' services such as Christmas and Harvest and Remembrance or whatever.

I also think there will inevitably be larger and larger groupings of churches. Perhaps most churches will have their own local priest with pastoral care of his/her own parish and leading occasional services, but there might be only one or two regular major services from a central point, internetted.

And perhaps people will feel more able to be open about their faith. If we begin to worship at least part of the time by logging on to an interactive service from home, there should be more open discussion of spirituality with fewer 'experts' telling people what they ought to think. People will be encouraged to follow their own path.

I also think the major faiths will have to find some common ground and work on it, so that all spirituality can eventually kind of gather under one large umbrella. Not that I think worship will be identical or religions identical. Today different Christian denominations live reasonably happily together; in the same way the world's faiths will be able to co-exist, recognizing one God but different ways of meeting him. And we'll begin to borrow a bit more from each other's faiths. But that may be more like 100 years away!

Reshaping a Tradition

These impressions of fresh springs in English parishes do not deny that there are major challenges: smaller congregations, fewer full-time ministers and many financial problems. But all are making changes. One of these communities saw itself in Old Testament terms. After the conventional regularities of life in Egypt came all the surprises of existing in a desert. The stories of the burning bush and the prophetic criticism of temple worship affirmed the faith in new surroundings. The divine is seen in something which is consumed but not destroyed, something which is believed to glow more brightly, as in the Bible story of the burning bush. What the members of these changing parishes are coming to believe is that the principles of the Bible story of death and resurrection must be woven into the healing and learning process of their searching pilgrimage.

The life of the church in these small communities, both in country and city, depends on the faithfulness, imagination and conviction of many clusters of individuals. The women and men who minister, whether lay or ordained, give the groups the ability to express themselves, articulating their needs and hopes. Sometimes the leaders are well known, as in the villages round Wormingford on the Suffolk–Essex border, where the Reader is Ronald Blythe. More often the core groups, committed to the gospel and to worship, are enabled by the ministers to be leaven in the community, not widely recognized but working away, and known always to God.

References

Blythe, Ronald, *Akenfield*. London, Allen Lane, 1969.

Blythe, Ronald, *Out of the Valley: Another Year at Wormingford*. London, Viking, 2000.

Blythe, Ronald, *Word from Wormingford: A Parish Year*. London, Viking, 1997.

Jowett, Nicholas, 'Hope Within a Broken Church' (*Guardian*, 5 February 2000). Also private correspondence and conversation.

Milford, Catherine, private correspondence and conversation.

Scott, Janice, private correspondence and conversation.

3 NORWICH CATHEDRAL: Discovering Fresh Springs

What time disfigured, turned to dust,
We have renewed, as Christians must
Who hold faith's heritage in trust:
  Alleluia!

Now to God's glory, we must prove
This is the base from which we move
To do his waiting tasks of love:
  Alleluia!

So may the living Church, restored
In mind and spirit by her Lord
Not only speak but live his Word:
  Alleluia!

(From the hymn written for the 1975 Restoration
Thanksgiving by Fred Pratt Green)

When Alan Bennett gave his lecture entitled 'Comfortable Words' on
the English Prayer Book, he confessed that much as he admired
Cranmer's style as compared with modern services, he hesitated
about the Prayer Book being described as 'heritage'. When he shrank
from the 'kiss of peace' in the new communion services, he wondered
if his hesitation was due to his own snobbery. He asked whether the
curate going up in the lift to the fourteenth floor of a tower block in
a slum parish, trying not to breathe in the stench of urine, really
needed to bother about the language of the liturgy. Did Cranmer die
for English prose?

Alan Bennett's question about heritage is probing. *Heritage and
Renewal* is the title of the report by the Archbishops' Commission on

Cathedrals published in 1994. George Bernard Shaw's snide remark, pointing to the alleged élitism of cathedrals, was 'Are they not God's country houses?' But if cathedrals were built to symbolize, to actualize the divine presence in humanity, how should they behave and what is their record?

The walls of cathedrals and the lives of the communities which staff them and worship there either occasionally or more regularly prove that modern life is not placid as in a Barchester novel by Anthony Trollope or in an 'All Gas and Gaiters' comedy. The memorials around Norwich Cathedral record grim facts about East Anglian life and death. There are long lists of those killed in South Africa, the names of bloody battles in Europe and the East in two world wars, and other inscriptions which remind us of bitter events: gassing in Flanders and obliteration bombing throughout Europe, the losses on the Burma railway and in Korea. But some events are ignored – the 200 killed in the April 1942 air raids on the city, the harsh slums and destructive unemployment and low farm wages are unrecorded. While immense efforts were made to restore the incomparable bosses in the cathedral and cloister roofs, was there too much stress on heritage and not enough empathy for human suffering?

At virtually every communion service since 1662 the celebrant prayed that the lives of all those present might be a 'reasonable, holy and lively sacrifice'. It is fair to assess the quality of the life of the cathedral in terms which clergy and congregation were themselves using Sunday after Sunday. How alert were cathedral activities to the realities of life in the cities and the countryside? Were they in danger of confining themselves to the conservation of a building and to traditional liturgy?

In 1896 Norwich Cathedral was 800 years old and tried to assess itself. The fabric was in a better state of repair than it had been for several generations. There was alert, compassionate and un-snobbish leadership. Dean William Lefroy was brought up in Dublin, became a journalist, took a degree by evening study and after ordination proved himself to be an outstanding preacher and administrator. He had been brought to Norwich after creating the organization and finance for the Anglican Diocese of Liverpool. He reacted against the quiet and seclusion of the Close, which he described as an 'ecclesiastical Elysium'. He founded nave services, which attracted congregations of a thousand or occasionally two thousand on Sunday evenings. He ended the system for pew rents for the morning services, which allocated proprietary pews for residents of the Close. He was particularly friendly to Free Church people and insisted that, though episcopacy could be an asset to a church, it was not essential to the gospel itself. He raised funds on a large scale for many good secular causes – the Jenny Lind Hospital, Norwich School and other social and educational needs. Even on holiday he continued his fund-raising efforts by building a new English church at Riffelalp above Zermatt and another at Adelboden. He led an appeal in Switzerland for the relations of guides killed in a climbing accident. Lefroy was the only Dean whose sermons at Norwich, in London and in the United States were published in book form. A window in the nave and alpine flowers carved on his memorial stone testify to the influence and popularity of this attractive character.

Lefroy was a realist. Preaching in London, only a few years before World War I, he was rebuked by the press for a doom and gloom sermon at the Chapel Royal. The critic wrote: 'When the Dean next comes, let him see if he can be more triumphantly eloquent by assuring us, as any man can see who does not go through life with his eyes shut, that the world is growing better.' The cautious Dean of Norwich had the shrewder judgement. He was the only non-Oxbridge Dean of Norwich during the past century and was determined to open the cathedral to the community. In his own words: 'Cathedrals reflect the past, recognize the present, they believe in the future, to discover the best and to meet the needs of the present day.' It even came to be believed that King Edward VII asked for a telephone to be installed in the cathedral pulpit so that he could listen in when he was in Sandringham to Dean Lefroy's sermons!

The celebrations in 1896, the Eighth Centenary, gave the cathedral new confidence. The sermons show that the church was coming to terms with the teaching of Darwin (though the issues raised by Marx and Freud and the technology of science lay ahead). It felt confident enough to try to raise large sums of money for non-church causes. It was deeply involved in the community and behaved as one might expect of the Church of England, giving a lead over the educational and social needs of the community, concerned for everyone of all classes.

1900 Onwards

How unforeseen and tragic were the following 100 years with the trauma of two world wars. The religious world was to change almost beyond recognition. Many people now rejected religion and the Church of England found itself in danger of being isolated. Sections within the Church of England turned away from reunion with the Free Churches. Social life was transformed and Sunday with it. Increasingly Sunday became the day for relaxation, sport and shopping, and thus a working day for thousands. But the city is better educated, clothed and fed and has better health services and longer holidays than in the past centuries. There is still insecurity about jobs but many of the changes made have been on the side of justice, caring and happiness.

The City of Norwich Plan 1945 by C. H. James and Rowland Pierce, an impressive wartime document, was researched and written while the city was still being bombed. It quotes Winston Churchill's famous challenge: 'We have one large immediate task in the replanning of our cities and towns.' In addition to the destruction by bombing of considerable areas within the city, there was a crisis on the roads with mounting numbers of accidents and traffic confusion. Norwich owes much to the stimulus of the bold and imaginative approach, which the 1945 Plan brought to the city's problems. The planners considered the cathedral and the area around it, including the bishop's garden and the public space around Cow Tower at the back of the Great Hospital. Their recommendations of more land for Norwich School were ignored but major efforts cleared most of the slums and the re-housing projects were a triumph of local government.

In 1972 the Lord Mayor and the Dean together increased public accessibility to the Close with the opening of the Riverside Walk. A moving Remembrance Day service with prayers led by a German lecturer and a challenging sermon by the visionary housing reformer Richard Carr-Gomm led to the founding of an Abbeyfield House in the Close and of the St Matthew's Housing, which now provides homes for 500 people in Eastern England. The opening in the Close of Centre 71 with a meeting room, library and canteen, where social and spiritual problems could be addressed, facilitated co-operation between the city, the churches of all denominations and the cathedral. In the vestry of a redundant church a Night Shelter was opened, staffed at first by young lawyers, clergy and businessmen and women. Today the shelter, renamed the St Martin's Society, has expanded greatly, with purpose-built accommodation for 100 each night and other services for the homeless. The foundations of all this work were laid by a Norwich housing estate curate who spent every night for a month being alongside and making friends with the bedless in porches of shops and churches or on bombsites.

The cathedral Close may seem a far cry from these concerns. But a survey of the social work undertaken by its residents would be impressive. And though many citizens and tourists who lunch on the grass during the summer will realize that the Close provides essential space in the centre of the city, they are probably not aware of its extent. It is one of the largest Closes in England, 40 acres with 90 dwellings, 24 offices, Norwich School and its playing fields.

If the Close remains relevant for the life and hopes of the city, then without doubt the Close will adapt to new needs. Now £10,000,000 is being raised for a major renovation of cathedral facilities for education, music, exhibitions and refreshments. In co-operation with the University a Sainsbury Institute of Japanese Art and Culture is to be opened in the Close.

But the cathedral still provides essential and life-giving space. When the Lord Mayor's Procession, in all its lively confusion, ends at the Close and hundreds stream into the cathedral, then there is a realization of what the Victorians like to call, in a moving though sentimental vision, Mother Church opening her arms to her children.

It is, however, easy to exaggerate the sense in which the cathedral is a religious home to Norfolk people. In 1963, of eight men working on a farm in central Norfolk, only two had ever been to Norwich, let alone the cathedral. Today the one worker, in his sixties, goes to Norwich 'never hardly' and has only once been to a service at the cathedral – because his mother was carrying the Mothers' Union banner, and he 'watched from the top'. There are no statistics about visits from the city, but an informed guess suggests that less than 10 per cent of the population of the city has ever entered the Close or the cathedral. If 'the Close' is to become 'the Open', imaginative welcoming events are needed for young people and today's Education Officer and volunteers certainly enable this work.

The cathedral has tried to serve the city by teaching and preaching, aiming at revealing the relevance of faith in a rapidly changing society. In the eighteenth and nineteenth centuries Norwich was the home of many radical thinkers, both in politics and religion. Norwich and Norfolk pioneered the formation of agricultural unions, which applied teachings about justice and fairness inherited from the Christian faith. Church people, however, often saw the unions as hostile. Relationships with the farming community were disrupted by disputes over tithes on land paid to the Church of England.

Dean Lefroy had been especially concerned with economic justice. He had questioned the occasions when the stock exchange system was abused. He stressed the need for regulation, particularly in dealing with futures. He noticed the crimes of bankers when savers and pensioners were defrauded. He emphasized the changes needed in our understanding of Christianity once we have grasped the fact that the majority of all human beings have never even heard the name Jesus Christ.

Other Deans, particularly Dean Willink and Dean Norman Hook, addressed these problems. Dean Willink was a diligent and friendly pastor visiting all over the city and appointing colleagues devoted to the welfare of young and old. In Willink's day the Chapter had a reputation of being reliable friends for anyone in trouble. The size of the nave service congregations and the wording of his memorial in the nave testify to his attention to the realities of Norwich life.

Episcopal leadership was not always so sensitive. But this changed in 1959 when a scientist and Antarctic explorer, Launcelot Fleming, was appointed Bishop. If the medium is the message, Fleming's characteristics reinterpreted the Church – no longer distant but friendly. Fleming had been a Cambridge don, tutor in geology and rowing coach. As an ordination candidate he told his bishop that he did not believe every single statement in the Creed was literally true; some were symbol or metaphor. The son of an Edinburgh GP, he liked discovering things for himself. So in Norfolk he paid visits to many country vicarages, and at first hand – unlike some of his predecessors, who had usually stayed with the squire – he saw the depression, poverty and isolation of many parsons and their families. In one vicarage the guest room bed was so cold and damp that he had to change back and sleep in all his clothes.

Fleming's friendliness put him alongside young and old in the city and county. He was a keen games player – hockey, squash, tennis and rowing. He was encouragingly outspoken. He stood publicly against Enoch Powell's attack on black immigrants. He spoke frequently, both in Norfolk and in the House of Lords, against factory farming. He led efforts to control the exploitation and pollution of the oceans, and was personally involved in efforts to protect the polar regions, as earth's last great wildernesses. His biography shows him stripped to the waist, standing in a pool in an Antarctic ice floe.

When Fleming preached to the British Association meeting in Norwich he discussed the relationship between scientist and believer and suggested that the scientist must be detached in evaluating the results of his or her experiments, but in relationships he or she must be committed. As he grew older, and the speed of scientific discovery increased, Fleming was more and more concerned to preach an open, undogmatic Christianity. He was also not embarrassed to preach on the vital need for friendship and committed relationships in all communities, both scientific and religious.

This faith was reflected in his policy for the city and diocese, which led to his creation of teams and groups, specialist ministries for industry, education, youth, TV and major Norwich and Norfolk interests. He encouraged the cathedral to press ahead with inviting lay groups to consider political and religious problems in its Friday Forums. He insisted that the churches were not concerned with preaching a set of propositions, but with the creation of a pattern of relationships, clear, calm and lucidly reasonable.

The city responded to this fresh approach. Two ministers, an Anglican and a Methodist, succeeded each other in 1988 as Sheriff of the city, a ceremonial officer serving with the Lord Mayor. The city expected the Church to have a strong involvement in Norwich and Norfolk life: here was evidence of the effectiveness of that link. Raymond Frostick, a Lord Mayor who belonged to Princes Street United Reformed Church, noted the change in relationship and on one occasion, with his minister Donald Hilton, led the congregation in a robed procession from their church into the cathedral. The Anglicans remembered with penitence the exclusion of dissenting ministers by the Act of Uniformity on St Bartholomew's Day in 1662. There was a healing of memories and a new resolution to work together.

Founding a University

The foundation of a university at Norwich had been mooted for many years. Sir Eustace Gurney, Lord Mayor in 1910, had first talked of it but the university was not opened until 1963. It was fortunate that Launcelot Fleming became Bishop in 1959 as plans were being finalized. The first office for the as yet unborn university was in the Close. Many at the cathedral had hoped that the university would be founded in the centre of Norwich and felt that the Vice Chancellor should be a Christian. Others had suggested that there should be a service of dedication, and plans for this were drawn up. Some hoped for a theological faculty, others for a prominent chapel and chaplaincy, and for the strong establishment of the churches within the campus. All these suggestions were difficult in the England of the sixties. There was no agreement as to whether there should be a chaplaincy centre, and the title 'chaplain' was objected to by some members of the Senate ('delegated representative' was preferred). Knowing that there had been resignations at Churchill College, Cambridge when a donor presented the new college with a chapel, some Senate members hoped for a university without the quarrels and disputes that they associated with organized Christianity.

Bishop Fleming was the ideal representative of the churches. He understood a university atmosphere, he was a scientist, he was thoroughly ecumenical, he was willing not only to give time to committees but also hospitality to the students, sharing their interests and playing frequent games of squash. Members of the Senate warmed to him personally.

The university chaplaincy was not opened until 22 January 1972. By this time Launcelot Fleming had left Norwich and his successor, who was less ecumenical and spoke and voted against the Anglican Methodist scheme, felt that he could not attend the dedication service at the centre, perhaps because an Asian graduate student read a passage from the Qur'an. It was agreed that the chaplaincy should have no symbols distinctive of any denomination, and should always be open to non-believers for any activities they wished. Only later did the Senate grant the use of the words 'chaplaincy' and 'chaplain'. But in 1963 a carol service had been held and services had begun in 'the Village' so that from the inception of the University, Christians joined together for worship, prayer and discussion of their faith, the denominations co-operating with each other.

Fleming was a lightning conductor, explaining to traditionalist Christians that this way ahead was theologically valid. He was aided by Professor Norman Sheppard FRS, and by Sir Bernard Feilden who had succeeded the original architect, Sir Denys Lasdun. Others who were strongly supportive were Professor Roy Campbell, a Presbyterian; Professor Marcus Dick, philosopher and atheist; Charles Jewson, a Baptist, and the first Vice Chancellor Frank Thistlethwaite, a Congregationalist with Quaker sympathies. At the opening of the building the Vice Chancellor described it as a 'modest but confident venture in the life of the Spirit'.

The moral of this co-operation with the city and the university suggests that the church can only give reasonable service if it is prepared not only to listen to the questions which are actually being asked by the society in which it lives, but also to rethink how it states its faith. The habit of dogmatically restating propositions from the past may not be as reasonable as some religious people claim.

Wholeness and Holiness

In the last hundred years, thousands of Norfolk and Norwich people have been glad of this special space within the city for prayer, meditation and recreation, and glad too that the spire of the cathedral, that astonishing achievement, has remained visible – a hint both by day and night of something beyond. The delicate flying buttresses, the soaring spire, the sense that stress lurks in every stone, all point to the risks of faith. Jack Burton, the Methodist minister who drove buses in Norwich for many years, has described in his *Transport of Delight* how much this holy building means to him. Holy buildings are ambiguous. The prophet Jeremiah warned his compatriots against trusting in the holy temple of Jerusalem (Jeremiah 7.4) and Jesus Christ said much the same. The twentieth-century Jewish philosopher Martin Buber has spoken of holy insecurity. Others have used the word *liminality* – standing on the border of new perceptions. The cathedral is a place where boundaries are crossed, where there are hints of another kind of life hidden in our familiar experience. This approach sees the cathedral and those who serve it as a centre, which cares for people affected by the rapid changes in our scientific but anxious age.

The classic work *The Idea of the Holy* by Rudolf Otto uses the old phrase that 'holiness is a mystery which both creates awe and also paradoxically attracts us'. There have been instances in the past hundred years where the cathedral has pointed effectively to the quality of holiness in contemporary life. On a May evening in 1919 when the working day was over, the body of Edith Cavell, after the funeral service in Westminster Abbey, was brought from Liverpool Street to Thorpe Station. No event in the religious history of the last hundred years in Norwich has drawn so many men and women, but especially men. Ten thousand lined the route in Prince of Wales Road to the cathedral and many thousands crowded the cathedral and the Close. An unedited film record shows that despite all the orderly arrangements of the establishment, military, municipal and ecclesiastical, the people of Norwich and Norfolk swamped the proceedings. Edith Cavell was both a heroine and a victim of war. Guilt and horror at the past four years was widespread. Edith Cavell was not a particularly privileged person, just a rather difficult vicar's kid from Swardeston, with a brother working for the Norwich Union. Here was a person to whom everyone could relate, her funeral a kind of post-war trauma therapy.

The Norfolk nurse in a bullet-ripped uniform was strange and yet compelling. Like Joan of Arc before her she was, for some, a heretic. She insisted on doing her own thing. Her final words were: 'Standing as I do in the sight of God and Eternity I know that patriotism is not enough, I must have no hatred for anyone.' These were words too challenging to be inscribed immediately on her statue in London. They had to wait four years for a change of government. By joining in this funeral people could experience release from a nightmare time that patriots saw as a climax of British achievement. So the coffin was carried through the cathedral, past the altar cross and buried in Life's Green.

Hundreds of thousands of words have been read, preached and sung in Norwich Cathedral in the last hundred years. How many of them have been remembered as holy and inspired and life changing? When I asked young people, some remained in their memory. In 1970, the story of the Good Samaritan was read by a ten-year-old at a major service arranged by Dr Lincoln Ralphs for colleges and schools to commemorate the 1870 Education Act. This small boy, rehearsed and quietly confident, stood in the high nave pulpit and read that unforgettable story about the man who fell among thieves and was ignored by the clergy but rescued by the Samaritan. Looking up, apparently knowing the passage by heart, the boy with his strong Norfolk voice faced the congregation – 'Go and do thou likewise'.

Norwich School holds its daily assemblies in that nave. In the eighties the then headmaster, Philip Stibbe, told the school the story of the Chindits in the Burma jungle and in particular of a severely wounded officer cared for by a young Burma rifleman, Maung Tun. The officer would have died if the Burmese had not stayed behind to care for him. When captured by the Japanese the Burmese man refused to reveal where the officer was hidden and was brutally killed. The Headmaster said from the pulpit: 'I was that young officer . . . I cannot put into words what I feel about that man . . . as long as I live I shall always have the feeling that my life is not my own.' His words were never forgotten and the story has been repeated again and again. These words have the quality of holiness.

Words gain a new resonance by being sung. This happened at the memorial service for Brian Runnett, a brilliant young organist who was killed in a road accident just when cathedrals were beginning to recognize his talents. It was a September evening in 1970, when East Anglian light was shining almost horizontally through the windows of the Cathedral nave, which was packed, especially with young people. Peter Pears had chosen an Appalachian folk song, a favourite of Brian Runnett's. He sang it after the blessing without accompaniment, his voice perfect, the words circling around the clerestories in nave and choir. People listened, elevated and mesmerized: 'I wondered as I wandered under the sky, why Jesus my saviour, he had for to die.'

No discussion of holiness can focus only on words and events: the cathedral can speak to people through silence. The power of silence is being discovered and rediscovered, whether in candle-lit cloisters or in the quiet of a contemplative prayer group in a secluded chapel.

Reasonable, Holy . . . and Lively?

Over the centuries Norwich Cathedral's liveliness graph would show troughs and peaks. Dean Lefroy had his difficulties with a very conservative Chapter and the first Nave Services on Sunday evenings had to be held in the Agricultural Hall. At the same time some at the cathedral seem to have been little concerned with the community, though Dean Goulburn saved the Close and the city from the plan to take the Lynn and Fakenham railway through the precincts – a case of conservation not unmixed with self-preservation. But unnecessary anxieties over links with City Hall could persist. When one Lord Mayor, both devout and scholarly, expressed a wish to read the lesson at the annual civic service, the Dean said he could not accede to the request in case there might one day be a Lord Mayor not so well qualified – a classic case of better-not-ism, and the old fear of setting a precedent.

The cathedral has often found it difficult to relate to the political and social life either of the city of Norwich, perhaps more radical, or of Norfolk, perhaps more feudal. It was a tragedy that both social attitudes and a mistaken theology prevented the cathedral authorities from recognizing how unjust were the conditions of life in so many villages. During much prophetic preaching at the cathedral on controversial themes, there seems to have been no support for the Primitive Methodists or for the trades union movement in their efforts to raise the living standards of the poorest agricultural workers, whose wages, housing, education and medical care were often deplorable, despite the best efforts of some doctors, teachers and country parsons.

The Bishop of Norwich and the cathedral clergy appear to have been unconcerned when the Rector of Burston, a village near Diss, as chairman of the school governors sacked the headmistress, despite the fact that she was a brilliant and most devout teacher. Her real offence was that her husband was an influential trades unionist. The children went on strike, and the parents set up a school on the green, gaining the support of George Edwards, who afterwards became the first Norfolk farm worker to be elected to Parliament. Both diocese and cathedral ignored this crisis. George Edwards was a Primitive Methodist, regarded by some at the cathedral as theologically and politically unsound. He was convinced that the weekday meetings to gain justice for the Burston headmistress and for the grossly underpaid farm labourers were as religious as the services he took in the Primitive Methodist chapels on Sunday. Perhaps the cathedral clergy were just too far away from him, a farm worker who started as a crow scarer at the age of six, was taught to read in his twenties, by his wife, and after a long, honourable and deeply religious political career was awarded the CBE. Only then did the bishops of the Established Church approach him to become a member of the Industrial Christian Fellowship. At so many points Anglican clergy ignored the struggle for justice: at one of Edwards' meetings, a local vicar actually offered to fight him, and was knocked down.

Another low point in the life of the cathedral between the wars was when the national press gathered in the south ambulatory to report on the unfrocking of Harold Davidson, the Rector of Stiffkey, who had quarrelled with the squire and was accused of immorality in his relationships with women in London. He later became mentally unstable, and was killed as a public entertainer when a lion in a circus mauled him. People in Stiffkey said: 'Them in Norwich did our rector in.' The gentle, caring pastor, Dean Norman Hook (1957–70) tried to heal those harsh memories by removing the furniture of the Consistory Court out of the chapel where the judgement had been read, recreating it as a place of prayer.

During the 1970s the cathedral was fortunate that the Dean and

Chapter and the laity shared responsibility for its life, thinking and worship. A High Steward's Committee had been formed by Dean Holland (1947–52) to advise on fabric and finance. They included lay people representative of the county and city, irrespective of their denomination. The Cathedral Consultation, set up in the seventies, enabled members of the congregation to share in decisions about worship and future plans. The Visitors' Centre and Exhibition was planned by a working party meeting 'to give some insight and interpretation of Christian life, and the work of the cathedral past and present, *dynamic and developing*'. Sir Roy Strong, together with the cathedral architect, an artist, two leading public figures and the cathedral's first Visitors' Officer, Margaret Webster, worked on the planning, with the Dean and Vice-Dean, for three years.

The title of the exhibition, *Vision of God – A Search for Meaning*, reflected the conviction that visitors could be inspired by an 'attempt to point to vision and search over nine centuries'. The panels on the thinking of Darwin, Marx and Freud were found to be surprising and informative. So often exhibitions have concentrated on church or architectural history, when the unspoken question of visitors may be 'Does this building and its activities do anything real for us today – or is it just heritage?'

New facilities are now being planned, and there is plenty of lively service in the context of the cathedral itself – over 3,500 Friends who raise annually £200,000, and many give voluntary service in the refectory, the shop and in the cathedral. Thousands of young and old crowd the Christmas services, and communicant numbers have increased yearly since 1945. However, the massively attended Sunday evening service is a thing of the past. Special services of all kinds take place for civic or other occasions, all requiring preparation and consultation, none perhaps more impressive than the annual service remembering death on the roads, or the commemoration of crafts-men who gave the cathedral a new roof and the spire new security, or the ordination of 24 women deacons as priests in 1994. Today the cathedral has a girls' as well as a boys' choir, unlike many other cathedrals, but as yet no woman celebrates or preaches regularly on Sundays.

When the aim of a 'reasonable, holy and lively sacrifice' is lost, cathedrals have suffered severely. In Norwich in the Middle Ages, relationships between the city and the monks were clouded by bitter disputes. The monks charged high rents on their many estates. In 1272 fighting broke out, both citizens and monks were killed, much of the cathedral was burnt and 30 citizens were publicly hanged as exemplary punishment, by the orders of the King. Relationships did not recover for hundreds of years. During the seventeenth-century Civil War, soldiers and citizens destroyed windows, statues, paintings and vestments in protest against what they saw as idolatrous worship. They have left a lead bullet embedded in an episcopal tomb – a salutary reminder that religion without justice and reconciliation can fuel conflict. In later centuries criticism of the cathedral took the form of just staying away.

The danger for all cathedrals is impersonal administration. Those who love cathedrals must maintain a superlative but fragile building and a liturgy beautiful in words and music but costly and time-demanding. There are the complexities of a large and changing community, many of whose hopes and enthusiasms can be contradictory. Clergy can become benign Pooh-Bahs, anxious about details – what to wear, where to sit and who processes in what order. Questions need to be asked about how much energy and time can be given to these concerns at the expense of being available to people, having time to listen, think and study. However, in practice cathedral congregations and clergy are often pioneers in working out fresh worship that meets contemporary needs, not least the demands of local or national voluntary societies.

Cathedrals always need the radical conscience of the young. When Norwich Treasury was built to display historic church silver from all over the diocese, it was the Young Friends of the Cathedral who argued that donations should be requested and given in their entirety to Christian Aid. They feared the cathedral might emphasize heritage and treasures and keep the money for itself. In 1981 Robert Aagaard, a Yorkshire layman, founded Cathedral Camps to invite young people to share the life of cathedrals for a week or a fortnight in the summer. His vision was to enable young people, in organized groups, under trained and responsible leaders, to undertake conservation work at cathedrals. More than 10,000, mainly British but including a number from abroad, have given their time, themselves paying a modest fee. They have worked in all English cathedrals and in some parish churches, as well as in Liverpool Metropolitan Roman Catholic Cathedral, some Free Churches and some cathedrals in Scotland.

Cathedral Camps has raised £100,000 each year to finance the work and maintain a small office. Grants are made to help volunteers who are disabled or unemployed, and campers are from many denominations or none. At times their work has been crucial: after the disastrous fire in the roof of York Minster, or helping Carlisle Cathedral to 'air' thousands of books in their library. The atmosphere of friendship and enjoyment has helped to enliven ancient buildings. Campers who vacuum the timbers inside soaring spires, clamber in their safety harness to cleanse clerestories, or sensitively wash Elizabethan chalices, grasp something of the skills and devotion of craftspeople of long ago as well as meeting the devotion of today.

Devotion, of course, can blow in on a side wind. In the seventies a major piece of co-operation between the cathedral and Norfolk Education Authority resulted in an exhibition 'One Thousand Norfolk Poets'. Schools were asked to encourage their children and young people to write a special poem – not about religion or even about the cathedral, but about whatever touched and moved them. All were exhibited, and drew in thousands from the schools, with parents and friends. There were Poetry Days, when the floor of the nave and the aisles were covered with children, either working in groups, or listening to comments and reflections by the poets Anthony Thwaite, Alan Brownjohn and Ronald Blythe.

We often find that the young can give us different and more hopeful perspectives. In 2000 a huge tapestry was created by primary schools in England. It is thought to be the longest tapestry ever made, over a mile long and involving over 300,000 children. It expressed what children found fun: football and other games, film stars and baked beans, holidays and the joy of colour, Nativity plays and their own homes. Norwich Cathedral could only display one tenth of the tapestry, but parents, friends and other visitors crowded in after seeing the tapestry on television. It felt as if the young were saying to the cathedral: 'Oh come on, cathedral, let us lead you into the future.'

Norwich Cathedral and its elegant Close, fine city and sea-girt county are a gracious heritage. The present generation is determined to cherish, extend and enjoy this treasure. Like all cathedrals its vocation is to pray and to care, sensitive to the needs of all who come – schoolchildren, institutions, tourists and worshippers. Its task is well described in two prayers that catch this spirit:

FOR THIS CATHEDRAL WITH ALL GOD'S PEOPLE

One thing we ask of you, Lord of all, one thing we need: to see your beauty and faithfulness in the land of the living. Live gloriously in this church, as in the activity, suffering and prayer of your whole creation; that in the silence and energy of your presence we may work with you, Father, Son and Spirit, to restore the hope and glory, always old and always new, which is your gift, your will, and our happiness. *Amen.*

FOR HUMAN NEED

Our times are in your hand, O Lord our God, our hope in your steadfast mercy. Set your healing to work in our sickness, your deliverance in our imprisonments, your light in our darkness. With the fire of your Spirit give us freedom to work and praise, that we may approach the future with open confidence: for it is yours and we are yours, dead and living together. We pray this in the power of your servant and our master, Jesus Christ. *Amen.*

(Two prayers written by John Drury, later Dean of Christ Church, Oxford, for the 1975 Restoration Thanksgiving)

References

Atherton, Ian, and others, eds., *Norwich Cathedral: Church, City and Diocese, 1096–1996*. London, Hambledon Press, 1996.

Bennett, Alan, *Writing Home*. London, Faber and Faber, 1994.

Burton, Jack, *England Needs a Revival*. London, SCM Press, 1995.

Burton, Jack, *Transport of Delight*. London, SCM Press, 1976.

Clark, Jean, *Change is Boundaries Dissolved*. Jean Clark, 1988.

Edwards, George, *From Crow-Scaring to Westminster*. London, Labour Publishing Co., 1922.

Leeds, Herbert, *Life of Dean Lefroy*. Norwich, H. J. Vine; London, Jarrolds, 1909.
Lindsay, Donald, *Friends for Life: a Portrait of Launcelot Fleming*. Seaford, Lindel, 1981.
Stibbe, Philip, *Return to Rangoon*. Barnsley, Leo Cooper, Pen and Sword Books, 1995.
Thistlethwaite, Frank, *Origins*. Frank Thistlethwaite, 2000.
Wren, Brian, *What Language Can I Borrow?* London, SCM Press, 1989.

Information also received from Gordon Tilsley OBE, Town Clerk of Norwich 1959–80; Derek Pearce, Oaks Farm, Kerdiston; and Norman Sheppard FRS, Professor of Chemical Sciences at the University of East Anglia 1964–81.

The address of the Cathedral Camps is: 16 Glebe Avenue, Flitwick, Beds MK45 1HS. They have a website, http://www.cathedralcamps.org.uk

4 PEOPLE AT ST PAUL'S

London thou art the flower of cities all.
(William Dunbar ?1465–?1530)

The community responsible for the worship and maintenance of St
Paul's Cathedral has lived through many changes since the first
Saxon building was set up on Ludgate Hill. There were critical
moments: the Norman Conquest, the creation of the great Gothic
complex of Old St Paul's, the Reformation changes, the Commonwealth abolition of the Chapter and the rebuilding after the fire by
Christopher Wren. In the nineteenth century Jeremy Bentham urged
that cathedrals should become Mechanics' Institutes, but instead
major reforms were carried through and cathedrals in a different
way flourished again as places of worship and prayer. World War II
was threatening with incendiaries falling on the Dome and two
500-lb bombs piercing the roof. The St Paul's Watch, of Londoners
young and old, saved the building during the Blitz, encouraged by
Dean Matthews, who had just lost his beloved son in the Navy and
spent many nights sharing the Watch. The twenty-first century
begins with the implementation of new thinking, which should
enable clergy and laity, men and women, to take responsibility for
the worship and life of the cathedral.

In Anglo-Saxon times at St Paul's the community had a written
rule, a historic and unusual document. The earliest written rule of
any cathedral in England, it reveals a group of canons living and
praying together, responsible for the life of the building but also,
like the Bishop of London at their head, involved in demanding
work right outside the cathedral complex. Some were monks, some
were celibate and some were married clergy, but the rule urged
them all to remember that prayer for London, early and late, was

their primary task. In the words of the rule: 'You shall consider that Paul is superior of you all by his calling in teaching and preaching. Do your service in the church in London and be content with the revenues assigned to you.' The rule went on to warn them against jealousy, whispering campaigns and mutiny. This Anglo-Saxon rule is direct, pious and shrewd as though foreseeing the struggles and temptations which the community of St Paul's would experience later when it had to fulfil its vocation wedged between Fleet Street, the Old Bailey and the City.

The Normans tightened the letter of the law at St Paul's. They appointed a dean, and the papacy insisted on celibacy, centralization and obedience to Rome. However, the members of the chapter remained independent and at their worst behaved like autocratic ecclesiastical barons. The years following the Norman Conquest were among the most disgracefully worldly in the long history of St Paul's. The managerial Normans began the process, which led to the erection of a court and a bishop's prison beside the cathedral. At the end of the Middle Ages in 1514 John Hunne, a London citizen with a lawsuit with the clergy over fees for the baptism of his son, was found hanged, murdered in the Lollards' Tower, the prison attached to the cathedral. The scholarly Dean, John Colet, who in a sermon to Parliament had criticized the clergy as living 'evil lives', so distrusted the unreformed chapter that he ensured that his cherished St Paul's School should be the responsibility of the laity – the Mercers' Company and not the chapter.

All communities, ancient and modern, suffer frustration when the strict letter strangles the spirit. Recent examples in museums, legal administration and journalism are all too public. In a lecture on 'Happiness' Sir Roy Strong has described the misery of trying to administer the Victoria and Albert Museum when the conditions seemed to be intolerable. The newspaper world has occasionally experienced stalemate. *The Times* in the nineteenth and twentieth centuries had close links with St Paul's (commemorating one of its proprietors, Lord Thomson of Fleet, with a tablet in the crypt describing him as 'a man from Nowhere', meaning that he was born in Manitoba – a rather London comment on a largish Canadian province). In the eighties the Editor-in-Chief, Sir Denis Hamilton, arranged a great artistic and devotional addition to St Paul's, Henry Moore's *Mother and Child*. But it was just in those creative years for *The Times* that a crisis arose and publication ceased for several months, owners were changed and new printing premises established. It was inspiring to be part of the planning for the installation of the *Mother and Child*, but painful to be alongside those newspapermen and feel their frustrations.

In 1998 St Paul's and other English cathedrals were promised a new, modernized structure of government, thanks to a commission chaired by Lady Elspeth Howe, a member of the then St Paul's Court of Advisors. This revision of the statutes aids the cathedrals, but Apostle Paul's abrupt sentence 'the written letters kill, but the Spirit gives life' (2 Corinthians 3.6, NJB) is still a wise warning. In managerial days it matters that we remember what the Spirit has contributed to the life of cathedrals. What the new Measure will do is 'to free from cathedrals the perception that their government is secretive, wholly clerical, unaccountable and unreformed', to quote David McClean, Professor of Law at Sheffield University, who moved the Measure in the General Synod.

Three notable servants of St Paul's, Ralph Inge, Richard Church and Sydney Smith, all groaned at the letter of the law of their times. Inge was so frustrated by his colleagues that he felt like a mouse watched by four cats. Richard Church wondered, when popular events and preachers filled St Paul's with thousands, whether they were addressing people's real questions. Sydney Smith endured a Dean who was an absentee Welsh bishop. The chapter wondered whether there was enough money or wood to make duck boards to bridge the rivers of mud which surrounded the cathedral. Sydney said: 'Let the Dean and Chapter lay their heads together and the thing will be done.' But as one head was at St Asaph it was easier said than done. The personalities and gifts of Inge, Church and Sydney Smith made a memorable contribution to the ability of St Paul's to serve London. Through their personal gifts, not least humour, learning, wisdom and determination to stand up for minorities, they helped to keep the church of their day in touch with reality.

Philosophy: Ralph Inge

Ralph Inge was Dean for 23 years (1911–34). As a Cambridge don he had achieved a memorable book entitled *Christian Mysticism*, arguing that the bedrock of religion was not the church or the Bible but mystical experience in prayer, God hidden in our minds and souls. Many found his gentle reasoned thesis deeply persuasive, especially when there were so many dogmatic divisions between churches.

Inge had a negative side. He was shy, rather deaf and often depressed. He disliked music, was short on small talk and could be sharp and brusque. If you mispronounced his name he would say: 'My name rhymes with "sting" not with "cringe".' The portraits show him tall and anxious, usually in a long black coat and gaiters. Like his friend Bernard Shaw he enjoyed shocking people. He debunked those who thought that the country was getting better and better to such effect that when Prime Minister Asquith appointed him to St Paul's, Londoners nicknamed him 'the gloomy Dean'. But he made a brave speech in 1917, the year of Passchendaele, a battle which cost nearly 400,000 British casualties. He foretold a second World War if nations continued to hate each other. But he never lost his wit, noting in his diary that among the abusive letters was one which ended: 'I am praying nightly for your death; I have been very successful in two other cases.'

He kept up an immense range of reading in English, French, German and the classics. His huge output of books, lectures and articles so captivated many who thought about their religion or politics that he received more attention throughout Britain than the utterances of Archbishops or Lambeth Conferences. Enjoying both the publicity and, critics hinted, the fees, this pillar of the establishment began writing two weekly columns in the *Evening Standard*. His gift for epigrammatic writing enabled him to speak to those on the margins as well as those in the pews. He understood that many Christians doubted the infallibility of the Bible and of the creeds and assessed bishops on their wisdom and humanity, not on their status. But he saw the difficulties of achieving a new understanding. 'The Englishman hates an idea he has never met before . . . and he takes opportunities of making things unpleasant for those who utter indiscreet truths.'

'We have not passed this way heretofore' were the words Inge used at the end of his 'Vale' summing up his own ministry. He was prescient. Every church today, including those with the most dogmatic hierarchies, is experiencing doctrinal and ethical questioning. Dietrich Bonhoeffer, Hans Küng, Tissa Balasuriya, Leonardo Boff, John Robinson, David Jenkins, Rosemary Radford Ruether, Monica Furlong and many others have been censured and later seen as prophets.

Inge welcomed the cumulative developments in science, based on the freedom to research and experiment. Medicine was not regulated 'by Thirty-nine Articles of physic' nor by creeds (which he defined as 'only the majority decisions of a Council'). He felt orthodoxy was hampered by regulation. He remarked that 'Faith makes many of the mountains which it has to remove'. Orthodox regulation of thought could inhibit adventurous inspiration and this could be fatal for any community which hoped to be joined by the next generation. 'The effect of boredom on a large scale in history is underestimated. It is the main cause of revolutions.' So he pleaded for 'latitude' – spaciousness, a tolerated variety of opinions in matters of belief.

Inge's experience of clerical life at St Paul's was traumatic. Chapter meetings were short on laughter, community feeling or a sensitive understanding of differences. If he was put down by his colleagues he would leave the Chair after a few minutes. Yet he was creative; in his time the dome was strengthened with grouting and hidden steel supports, which enabled it to withstand the Blitz. He welcomed the 1920 Lambeth Conference's positive decisions on the ministry of women. But his London contacts were limited. His major survey *England*, published in 1926, the year of the General Strike, showed him deeply critical of Labour aspirations. Dick Sheppard, the pastoral genius at St Martin-in-the-Fields, annotated his own copy 'undoubtedly the most depressing book possible'. Inge feared democracy and his son Richard had to teach him the virtues of those whom Richard served as a curate in Leeds and as an instructor in the RAF – an instructor so devoted that he gave his life at RAF Cranwell trying to rescue a trainee pilot from a blazing plane.

Inge's teaching encouraged questioners. 'Faith is not, as a school boy is reported to have said, believing what you know to be untrue. It is rather the resolution to stand or fall by the noblest hypothesis. It is an experiment which ends as an experience, a declaration of the intellect as well as the will, to the pursuit of all that is good and true.' His Christianity emphasized religious experience, its moments of transcendence. His thinking was in some respects parallel to that of Baron von Hügel – the Roman Catholic author of the seminal *The Mystical Element in Religion*. Inge, following the philosopher Plotinus, emphasized the hope of the vision of God.

He did not reject creeds but reinterpreted them.

An honest and reverent study of the New Testament will lead us to accept the orthodox view that in Christ 'abideth all the fullness of the Godhead bodily'. For a perfect revelation of the Divine under human conditions there must be a revelation of goodness, not power. That is a principle which carries us further than most of us have yet realised.

Since Inge's day New Testament scholars have continued their researches and in Britain, Europe and America the majority of these scholars suggest that many questions are unanswerable through lack of evidence. The New Testament both reveals and veils the mysterious wonder of Jesus Christ.

Inge suggested that

Churchmen who think for themselves are not traitors in the camp; they wish not to destroy but to rebuild what needs reconstruction; in a healthy religious society everyone should be encouraged to believe that part of the truth which he sees most clearly. For in a great Church all types of mind are represented. Some see one side of the truth, some another, and all sides should be fully expressed.

Inge's grief at the death of his daughter, and later his RAF son, was expressed in words which spoke to many. The strength of his faith can be sensed in the short booklet which Inge wrote about his daughter Paula (entitled *Personal Religion and the Life of Devotion*). He said:

> Bereavement is the deepest initiation into the mysteries of human life, an initiation more searching and profound than even happy love. Love remembered and consecrated by grief belongs more clearly than the happy intercourse of friends, to the eternal world; it has proved itself stronger than death. Bereavement is the sharpest challenge to our trust in God; if faith can overcome this, there is no mountain which it cannot remove. And faith can overcome it. It brings the eternal world more near to us and makes it seem real. It transports us into a purer air, where all that has been, is, and will be, lives together in its true being, meaning, and value, before the throne of God. The souls of the righteous are in the hands of God and what is dear to him will never be plucked out of the land of the living.
>
> By eternal life I do not mean merely survival in our time. The future has not been revealed to us. In this region we can only see as in a mirror, by means of symbols. But God has revealed Himself as love; and 'we know that we have passed from death to life because we love the brethren'.

The core of Inge's faith stood the test of time and remains crucial for the church today; the centrality of tolerance, the recognition of variety and the need for a personal faith almost unstatable in words. He acknowledged that in every age, if the gospel is to be believed and lived, it must be able to develop and absorb what is best in God's own developing world. The experiment of faith must be expressed by each individual personality and must satisfy their own mind and conscience. Inge never read Wittgenstein, but Inge's reticence, and moments of wordless faith, chime with Wittgenstein's insistence on silence on that of which one cannot speak.

Inge's biographer, Adam Fox, summed him up: 'This great lover of truth, ever grappling with it and with himself, so tormented, so irritable, so gifted, so intelligent, so dutiful, so affectionate, so unexpected, and all the time some kind of saint.' Wise churches will best serve the people of the future if they encourage wisdom, imagination, critical intelligence and reticence.

Wisdom: Richard Church

A generation before Inge came to St Paul's, Richard Church, slight, frail and sharp-featured, was appointed Dean (1871–90). He had been born in Lisbon and brought up in Florence in a family committed to the liberal cause in Europe. His uncle, an army officer, had been Generalissimo in the Greek War of Independence. At Oxford Richard Church had a wide range of friendships including John Henry Newman and scientists at the Oxford Observatory. As an exemplary country parson in Somerset he published regularly, especially on European and scientific themes, as well as on Anselm and Dante. He was happy as a country priest: Gladstone had the greatest difficulty in dragging him out to St Paul's, to live in what he called 'the gloomy magnificence of my decanal prison'.

> It is clear that what I am to come in for is very tough practical business . . . it is to set St Paul's in order as the great English Cathedral before the eyes of the country.

Reforming St Paul's was what he achieved, in stages, at a time when Queen Victoria had visited the cathedral and written in her diary (underlining the damning words), 'St Paul's is *dirty, dark* and *undevotional*.' Church could be over fastidious about the fabric, once astonishingly forbidding General Booth to bring his Salvation Army to church because they would scratch the marble floor with their hobnailed boots. He sympathized with ritualists and urged tolerance for Anglo-Catholic priests. He worked for peace and an end to ecclesiastical lawsuits.

Church, like Inge, was prepared to ask fundamental questions. Writing to his conservative colleague, Canon Liddon, the stirring preacher of the day, he remarked:

> Ever since I could think at all, I have felt that these anxious and disturbing questions would one day be put to us; and that we are

not quite prepared or preparing to meet them effectively... We have not adequately prepared to face things for ourselves, and in our own way, in order not merely to refute but to construct something positive on our own side.

It was easy to despair of institutional religion and resign from active concern with the churches. Criticism was intense. While Church was at school in Bristol the bishop's palace had been burnt by the mob. This crisis encouraged Church to ask awkward questions. Do we need an established church? His ancestors had been Quakers and he saw their point of view. Can there be any form of authority with ultimate validity other than rational persuasion? Had religion really grasped the implications of the gospel for relations between the sexes? Dean Church did not shout these questions from the pulpit but he was beginning to grapple with them and his influence with the religiously troubled or agnostic was due to his honest refusal to over-simplify. 'I do think', said Church 'that the time may be hoped for when a controversialist will think it his first duty to put himself as far as he can in his opponent's position, and understand what *he* understands, and feel what he feels.'

Dean Church made the Cathedral a more Christian centre, as well as a model for other cathedrals. Finances were reorganized after negotiation with the Ecclesiastical Commissioners, music and choir traditions reformed by the appointment of Sir John Stainer, minor canons appointed to do pastoral and educational work in neighbouring parishes and the distinguished group of residentiary canons, Gregory, Lightfoot and Liddon, co-operated fully in the reformation. New mosaics and a new reredos gave fresh sparkle to the East end. As Gladstone's friend and advisor on religious questions, Church was uniquely influential.

St Paul's led the cathedrals in removing railings, opening the choir to the congregation, standing up to anti-ritualistic riots and insisting that the cathedral was for London and not a private chapel for the dean and chapter, the musical establishment and an élite congregation. A fanatic threw the cross and candlesticks on the floor shouting 'Protestants to the rescue' until an energetic canon stuffed a handkerchief into the culprit's mouth. Social and pastoral engagements were unceasing but Church proved by his preaching, writing and counselling that a reasonable, humane, intelligent faith could be lived in the heart of London. He was committed to live out, in his own phrase, 'the serious love of the unseen Christ', transmuted into intelligent pastoral concern.

Gradually St Paul's developed the tradition of facing straight questions, welcoming those on the margins, listening, not denouncing. A hundred years later Mikhail Gorbachev, then Secretary of the Communist Party, paid a private visit to St Paul's and enquired from the Dean's Virger, 'What do you use the dome for?' He received the reply: 'Sir, to worship God.' Raisa went to look at the crib, the creation of the Polish artist Astrid Zydower, and was told its story. When students at the City University, for whom no accommodation was available, squatted in the Old Deanery in 1978 they were eventually and amicably persuaded to leave. On the old floorboards they left a farewell message in shaving soap: 'Thank you, dear house, for your beautiful vibes.'

John Betjeman, though no doubt he would have been anxious about squatters, would have approved of the inscription. He wanted to see church buildings as 'banks of affection'. He knew that the quiet atmosphere of all religious and cultural buildings in London could be threatened by financial stringency, tourism and sometimes impersonal management systems. Clergy are sometimes not available for shared prayer or for pastoral listening, such is the pressure of administration. The movement of the Spirit demands the commitment of laity and clergy, women and men, with time for others and for prayer, listening and reflection.

Wit: Sydney Smith

Forty years before Richard Church was appointed Dean, St Paul's received its most famous canon. Sydney Smith (1831–45) was unique: a priest, campaigner, journalist and wit, in whose honour an active association still holds regular celebrations. All his life he asked difficult questions. He was widely respected for his common sense and humour. When he was lecturing at the Royal Institution, on moral philosophy, the laughter could be heard in the street outside.

In a St Paul's sermon, when Nelson and Wellington were the heroes of the day, he wondered, did Britain have to be continuously at war – 35 minutes of every hour according to his calculations? In a review article he asked could the wealthy (whose delectable dinner parties he so enjoyed) stop using small children to sweep their kitchen chimneys? He tried to laugh people out of self-satisfaction and economic and political selfishness. He might have said with the twentieth-century Spanish writer, Miguel de Unamuno, 'God deny you peace and give you glory.'

Before he became Canon of St Paul's, Sydney Smith had been a Fellow of New College, Oxford, and a founder of a radical quarterly *The Edinburgh Review*. He had been tempted to give his life to the Law rather than the Church, but his father would not pay the fees for legal training. Sydney found himself, however, happy in the Church and in his relationships with people. His wit and jokes were so compelling that fellow guests at dinner were known to fall about and waiters to retire to the kitchen to recover. He fascinated children and was fascinated by them. He thought it was important to spend an hour a day 'romping' with his son and daughters. Seeing a child stroking the shell of a turtle he asked why. The child replied, 'To please the turtle.' Smith said, 'You might as well stroke the Dome of St Paul's to please the Dean and Chapter.' He loved London but was realistic about its shortcomings. 'He who drinks a tumbler of London water has literally in his stomach more animated beings than there are men, women and children on the face of the Globe.'

Sydney Smith believed that wit could move mountains – even long-established mountains. In the House of Commons it was being argued by Tories that to allow prisoners accused of felony to employ counsel would be a grave expense to the prisoner. Sydney parodied the politicians saying to the prisoner,

> You are going to be hanged tomorrow, it is true, but consider what a sum you have saved! Mr Scarlett or Mr Brougham might certainly have presented arguments to the jury, which would have secured your acquittal but do you forget that gentlemen of their eminence must be recompensed by larger fees and that if your life had been saved, you would actually have been out of pocket above

£20? You will now die with the consciousness of having obeyed the dictates of a wise economy; and with grateful reverence for the laws of your country, which prevent you from running into such unbounded expense – let us now go to prayers.

He laughed at reactionaries in the Commons and was even more effective when combating the House of Lords. The Lords had opposed the emancipation of Roman Catholics in Ireland and in the United Kingdom and also the Reform Bill. His longing for a simple form of religion, his concern to do good and be happy, were all offended by the injustice to those who were Roman Catholics who had no vote and no opportunity to hold public office or be commissioned in the Army. He did not fail to notice that it was the bishops who had defeated these measures. He liked to quote as an old saying, 'An ounce of mother wit is worth a pound of clergy,' and later commented: 'What bishops like best in their clergy is a dropping down deadness of manner.' He laughed at someone's élitist idea of heaven as eating paté de foie gras to the sound of trumpets.

His most famous story, in favour of widening voting rights, was Mrs Partington's battle with the Atlantic Ocean. With much drama, as though he was waving a mop and getting angrier and angrier as the rising tide poured in, he told a packed Town Hall at Taunton the story of the great storm from the Atlantic which finally overwhelmed Mrs Partington. He was confident that the need for Reform in the United Kingdom would overwhelm the House of Lords. Comparing the Lords to Mrs Partington he said:

I do not mean to be disrespectful, but the attempts of the Lords to stop the progress of reform reminds me very forcibly of the great storm of Sidmouth, and of the conduct of the excellent Mrs Partington on that occasion. In the winter of 1824 there set in a great flood upon that town – the tide rose to an incredible height – the waves rushed in upon the houses, and everything was threatened with destruction. In the midst of this sublime and terrible storm, Dame Partington, who lived upon the beach, was seen at the door of her house with mop and pattens, trundling her mop, squeezing out the seawater, and vigorously pushing away the Atlantic Ocean. The Atlantic was roused; Mrs Partington's spirit was up. But I need not tell you that the contest was unequal. The Atlantic Ocean beat Mrs Partington. She was excellent at a slop, or a puddle, but she should not have meddled with a tempest. Gentlemen, be at your ease – be quiet and steady. You will beat Mrs Partington.

Sydney Smith found the disagreements of the chapter at St Paul's as comic as the behaviour of Mrs Partington. Despite his 16 stone and double chin he was extremely energetic, climbing to the roofs and pushing himself through narrow openings. He said to a close friend: 'I am just going to pray for you at St Paul's, but with no very lively hope of success.' He radiated good nature and could not understand why small groups should be miserable and quarrelsome. He laughed at himself and believed that those who stood on their dignity would be left standing. He said, 'Life is to be fortified by many friendships . . . To love, and to be loved, is the greatest happiness of existence.' As a rural JP Sydney had been lenient with poachers and with the poor, the unfortunate and those who frequented alehouses.

The heart of Sydney's creed was that God is tolerant and that to know all is to forgive all. He distrusted the pride of cathedrals and churches. He felt that he must frighten off some of his friends from coming to St Paul's. The institution did not fit God's purposes, especially in winter.

To go to St Paul's is certain death. The thermometer is several degrees below zero. My sentences are frozen as they come out of my mouth, and are thawed in the course of summer, making strange noises and unexpected assertions in various parts of the church; but if you are tired of a world which is not tired of you, and are determined to go to St Paul's, it becomes my duty to facilitate the desperate scheme. Present the enclosed card to any of the virgers, and you will be well placed.

At St Paul's Sydney became a close friend of one of the minor canons, the author of *Ingoldsby Legends*, R. H. Barham, even though their politics were very different. Endlessly hospitable, he was active over his administrative duties; he was the first person to insist that an ecclesiastical building should be insured. He reorganized the musical foundation, installed mains water, some heating and gas lamps in the choir and insisted that the building should be cleaned. Sydney deplored, with his usual humour, his own impetuosity, as every aspect of the cathedral felt the animation of his energy. He quizzed everybody but hurt no one's feelings.

In hard times for society and religion, Sydney Smith insisted that laughter is used by the Spirit to keep us on our pilgrimage. Sydney laughed at himself and shared the pleasure with all around him. He was extremely well read but liked to pretend he was not. 'I never read a book before reviewing it: it prejudices a man so.' He suspected that he would not be a bishop because he was so independent – and so funny. Lord Melbourne, who reduced the young Queen Victoria to gales of laughter by repeating Sydney's jokes, regretted he never made Sydney a bishop. To the very end Sydney made new friends, including Peel, Disraeli and Daniel Webster, the American Secretary of State. He was endlessly generous to young authors – particularly encouraging Charles Dickens.

In his last years he became more conservative, opposed the reforming measures of Bishop Blomfield and the Ecclesiastical Commission, and was attacked by his critics as self-interested. To one of his friends who, like him, suffered from depression, he wrote: 'Make the room where you commonly sit, gay and pleasant. Be firm and constant in the exercise of rational religion.' He poured his spirit into his correspondence. As a friend wrote on a letter he had received: 'Dear Sydney – his conversation was still more racy than his writing. His spirit was more joyous than nature on a summer day.'

He shared his humour not only with the great and grand at Holland House but with those who worked for him at his country vicarages and their adjoining fields and in St Paul's. The essence of his Christianity was summed up in his maxim, 'Remember every person ... has rights and feelings. In all contentions let peace be your object rather than triumph: value triumph only as the means of peace.'

When Sydney Smith, Richard Church and Ralph Inge came to St

Paul's they had already won the gratitude of hard-pressed minorities. Sydney Smith was the champion of the children who climbed up London chimneys and of disadvantaged Roman Catholic clergy. Richard Church had supported democratic regimes in Europe and supported greater freedom for thought and worship in England. He had welcomed Darwin's work on evolution. Ralph Inge had written on behalf of those who found dogmatic religion unconvincing and had rediscovered the mystic Julian of Norwich. Later in the twentieth century Canon John and Diana (now Dame Diana) Collins did effective and heroic work in the struggles against the death penalty, nuclear war and, above all, against apartheid in South Africa. The courage, laughter, wisdom and mysticism of the communities of the past underpin hopes for the future.

Visitors and Pilgrims

Believers feel as if the Spirit was always on the move, slightly ahead. William Morris christened St Paul's 'God's railway station', intended in part as a rebuke for the general mêlée which the visitor might find. But it can serve those prepared to make a journey. Built on Watling Street, one of the main roads of Londinium, it stands firm at the heart of the City. Christopher Wren gave it a feeling of vibrant intensity, as though it was on the move like hurried commuters. The writer Sir William Rees-Mogg once commented that St Peter's, Rome, feels stationary, but St Paul's has a sense of movement, as if it was on a journey. When Sir James Thornhill painted his eight great themes of the life of St Paul in the dome, he chose the most dramatic moments to face the worshippers, the conversion of St Paul on the road to Damascus, his escape from the viper on landing on the island of Malta, and his trial before Festus and Agrippa which led to his removal to Rome and his eventual death. All are travel scenes.

Worshipping in St Paul's means joining people on the move. Congregations, once mainly British, coming to 'the parish church of the British Empire', are now international. Impressions indicate that at least half of many congregations come from abroad. Every Sunday morning is a fulfilment of the biblical prophecy, 'I shall gather them in from all the countries where I have driven them' (Jeremiah 32.37).

St Paul's is a pilgrim church rather than a church for an established community, though fortunately there are many for whom it is their 'parish church'. Modern communicators sometimes pay tribute to the genius of Wren. In 1981 when Alastair Burnet was preparing his TV commentary for the Royal Wedding, which was to be televised to most of the world, he said: 'One day, Dean, you will find the actual plans of Sir Christopher Wren, which will show precisely where he intended the TV cameras to be placed!'

Eleven years later when that marriage was in difficulties Princess Diana remembered going round one evening before the wedding. She wrote to me: 'Much has happened since our quiet walk around St Paul's, but I know you will understand that the most important thing I have learnt in that time is the strength which comes from sharing what happiness I can with those you call "on the margin". I simply want to do it better. Incidentally, I'm sure Julian of Norwich is right.' (This was a reference to Julian's words 'All shall be well', which appear on a banner in St Paul's.)

Perhaps the best impression of the needs of those who come to St Paul's is conveyed in the words of someone who for 20 years spent time caring for those around her in the cathedral. Preaching in St Paul's in 1992 Sister Hilary, of the Wantage Community, testified to the wish of so many visitors to share the reality of their lives, including their sufferings.

> Looking back over ten years as a member of the Pastoral Team of this Cathedral, I am struck by one fact. I must have met people from all continents and many of the countries of the world. The encounters I remember most sharply have been with people who have come here with heavy baggage – not so much the weight of their back-packs and hold-alls, but the burden of their lives, their relationships, their circumstances, their fears and troubles and anxieties. It soon becomes clear that the statistic of two million visitors a year does not reveal the whole story. People *do* come here as part of their tourist programme, but they also come here to be silent, to review their lives, to reflect and sometimes to weep. Once inside, the building moves them to share the problems and worries and sufferings.

There is a good deal in the readings and prayers for this particular Sunday (Pentecost 13) about SUFFERING – Christ's suffering, human suffering. I'd like to share with you how the ancient words of scripture have come alive in fresh ways, as strangers from far and near have been moved to open their hearts in this holy place, where prayer and worship are part of the fabric, as real as the mosaics in the ceiling, prayer which has gone on ceaselessly in the various churches on this spot since the seventh century.

There was the Afro-Caribbean woman, escaping in the lunch hour from the Old Bailey, where her teenage son was figuring amongst the accused in a notorious trial. She found some comfort in the Communion Service and went off down Ludgate Hill tearfully requesting prayers for her son.

There was the young Jewish pair, brother and sister, separated by strife for ten years in the Middle East. They had arranged by post to meet here, in this Christian building, and asked me to say with them prayers of thanksgiving that they had survived and found each other again.

There was the 14-year-old schoolgirl with leukaemia, on her way to St Bartholomew's Hospital for chemotherapy. She dreaded the side effects and was fearful that her life was slipping away too quickly. I wondered who was suffering the most, the daughter or her mother who was accompanying her. What had they hoped to find here? Did they find it?

There was the woman from Dresden, shortly after the Berlin Wall came down. In the middle of our conversation, she said to me totally without bitterness: 'I survived the Dresden incineration.' She was my age, and I could have been the person who survived – or did not survive – the Dresden carpet-bombing and firestorms, just before the end of World War II. She perceived my distress and put out a hand and said: 'Don't be upset – we did terrible things to your country also.'

There was the middle-aged epileptic woman, distressed, dirty and inadequately clad for a late winter afternoon. Clearly she had problems – drink, drugs, bereavement. She was wild and verbally abusive. Someone sent a virger to my rescue when it looked as though she might become physically violent. True, she had a roof over her head in north London, but that was about all – her one room was empty – no light – no heating – and the prospect of loneliness and a long dark night was too much for her.

There was the investigative journalist from Kiev, keen to learn how the UK coped with nuclear reactors. Some of her friends and relations in the Ukraine had died or become terminally ill as a result of the Chernobyl nuclear disaster.

Finally there was my recent encounter with a small Iranian Muslim girl from Hackney. She literally ran and skipped up to me under the Dome, and asked if she might listen to the next prayers. 'I believe in God, too,' she said, 'and I pray five times a day.' Then dark velvet eyes registered absolute unconditional acceptance of the differences between us – she had gone straight to the heart of what united us. Nothing else mattered.

These are instances of soul-meetings which may happen at any time in St Paul's. But moments of truth open up also through big occasions. Each year the Taizé Community holds a European meeting which gathers at least 25,000 young people from different parts of the world. From 29 December 1986 to 2 January 1987, Westminster Abbey, Westminster Cathedral, St George's Southwark, the Methodist Central Hall and St Paul's acted as hosts to the Taizé gathering which, for the first time, included 2,000 young people from Yugoslavia and 1,000 from Poland. The centres were linked by radio, and translations were provided. The parishes of London acted as hosts at night but the cathedrals were required, twice a day, to put themselves at the disposal of huge numbers. St Paul's moved most of its chairs so that the nave and dome and part of the transepts, uncluttered by furniture, could welcome those who came to pray, kneeling or sitting on the floor. The choir of about 100 singers and instrumentalists, directed by Brother Robert, in the south transept, and the Community gathered at the east of the dome, acted as a focus for the prayer and the music.

The Taizé brothers come mainly from the Protestant and Catholic churches, and their ecumenical aim has always been stressed by the Prior, Roger Schutz, himself a Swiss pastor. Preparations had gone on at St Martin-in-the-Fields since September, and gradually the

Community gathered until it transplanted itself almost entirely to London from its home at Taizé, a few miles from Cluny in Burgundy. The organization was impressive. Feeding points for the thousands of young people were provided beside St Paul's and elsewhere. There was a mingling of Christian insights and traditions. In St Paul's I noticed many Roman Catholic as well as Anglican priests, who had come from their parishes to join in the prayers, the music and the silence – simple, fluid and profound. *The Times* on 2 January commented:

> In Taizé, Protestant monks may assist their Protestant brethren to understand Catholicism better; and vice versa; and both to understand Christianity better, thus deepening their spiritual lives. What is outstanding about Taizé is that this message has spread all over Europe without any attempt by anyone to promote it or to evangelise in Taizé's name.

A rather impromptu supper in the Deanery with the Prior, Brother Roger, and 50 Brothers after the evening prayer on the last day of the old year was the climax for me. Some 9,000 had packed St Paul's to listen to their hopes for the new year, strengthened by the conviction that with God all things are possible. They prayed that one day the churches of the East, young people from Russia, even from China, would be able to worship with young people from the West. Pope John XXIII had discerned in Taizé 'that little spring time'. There is an unsatisfied hunger for the things of the Spirit that cathedrals, when they are open and adaptable, even on the most difficult days of the year, can nourish if the staff and congregations are themselves pilgrims, and at the service of pilgrims.

Today people will find more services at St Paul's than at any time since its foundation in the seventh century. The backbone of worship, both on weekdays and Sundays, is the Eucharist, Matins and Evensong. In addition every year there are hundreds of specially arranged services for national occasions, for the diocese, universities, colleges, schools and a great variety of charities. Many arise from a particular need; one evening during the hostage crisis in Tehran, hundreds of Americans in London came to St Paul's to pray. Soon afterwards their Thanksgiving Day service became another annual occasion when St Paul's was filled with worshippers.

But churches also try to serve those who come singly. One night in February 2001 a retired city businessman watched a TV programme on an archaeological dig in the crypt. The excavators found the body of a child, probably from the family of Christopher Wren's clerk of works. Like so many who have worked in the City all their lives, the businessman had never been inside St Paul's himself. He was moved by what he saw on TV, which included views of the recently installed dome altar. Here worshippers are together, in company with the clergy among them. These circles of worshippers symbolize and help to create prayer together for the Kingdom of God. The businessman caught an early train from his home in Gloucestershire to see what he had been missing. He came to the weekday Holy Communion service and talked afterwards, close to tears, with the priest who celebrated. So the ancient call to prayer for London continues in the twenty-first century. Even if the only link between many Londoners and St Paul's is the floodlit dome, now almost dwarfed by high-rise offices, it is still a reminder of the claims and values of faith and prayer, which are in no way foreign to our new multi-ethnic city.

Centuries ago John Donne had said 'Religion is a plural thing,' and had affirmed, in words now famous round the world, that 'No man is an island . . . any man's death diminishes me because I am involved in Mankind'. To be involved in humankind, not simply 'religious' humankind or 'Christian' humankind or 'English-speaking' humankind, is the hard vocation.

The cross on the dome of St Paul's stands hundreds of feet above the floor of the cathedral. The tradition is that Christopher Wren, standing in the ruins of Old St Paul's, called a workman to bring and lay before him a marker stone. From this, a stone from an old tomb, he began to make the measurements and calculations for the construction of the dome. As he was doing this he saw the inscription on the stone – *Resurgam*. I shall rise again.

Bring us, O Lord God, at our last awakening into the house and gate of heaven, to enter into that gate and dwell in that house,

where there shall be no darkness nor dazzling, but one equal light; no noise nor silence, but one equal music; no fears nor hopes, but one equal possession; no ends or beginnings, but one equal eternity; in the habitations of your glory and dominion, world without end. Amen.
(John Donne)

References

Bell, A. S., *Sydney Smith*. Oxford, Oxford University Press, 1980.

Church, R. W., published works.

Collins, Diana, *Partners in Protest: Life with Canon Collins*. London, Gollancz, 1992.

Dammers, Horace, ed., *Preaching from the Cathedrals*. London, Mowbray, 1998.

Fox, Adam, *Dean Inge*. London, Murray, 1960.

Matthews, W. R. and Atkins, W. H., *History of St Paul's Cathedral*. London, Phoenix, 1957.

Pearson, Hesketh, *The Smith of Smiths*. London, Hamish Hamilton, 1934.

Prestige, G. L., *St Paul's in its Glory*. London, SPCK, 1955.

Smith, B. A., *Dean Church*. Oxford, Oxford University Press, 1958.

Smith, Sydney, published works.

Details of the Sydney Smith Association are available from Major Peter Diggle, The Old Brewery, Thornton-le-Clay, York YO60 7TE.

5 FAITH IN THE CITY: Contemporary Prophecy

O God, open our eyes that we may see the need of others, open our ears that we may hear their cries, open our hearts so that they need not be without compassion. Let us not be afraid to defend the weak because of the anger of the strong, nor afraid to defend the poor because of the anger of the rich. Show us where love and hope and faith are needed, and use us to bring them to these places; through Jesus Christ our Lord.

(Alan Paton, the anti-apartheid campaigner, wrote this prayer which was used at the funeral of Giles Ecclestone, 1936–90, successively Clerk to the House of Commons, Secretary of the Board for Social Responsibility and a Cambridge country parson.)

The parable of the Good Samaritan ends with the incisive command 'Go and do the same yourself' (Luke 10.37, NJB). Christ is telling us to care for the abandoned, the victims of violence, the marginalized, all those beyond the fringe of comfortable society. But for Christian communities embedded in the established order of English life like the Church of England, in part financed from the distant past, often worshipping in expensive buildings, it is not easy to be Christian in the sense of sharing Christ's concern for the outsider. The Christ-like attitude is not the core of our normal business practice.

To face these claims, the Church formed groups of clergy and laity, often ecumenical, to think, research, consult and initiate action in line with that clear command 'Go, and do the same yourself'. When so many found themselves without work, homes, stable relationships, and education, church reports researched these traumas. Amongst these significant reports were *Family in Contemporary Society* (1958), *The Fourth R* (1970), *The Church and the Bomb* (1982), *Faith in the*

City (1985), *Not Just for the Poor: Christian Perspectives on the Welfare State* (1986), *Something to Celebrate: Valuing Families in Church and Society* (1996), *Unemployment and the Future of Work* (1997). These investigations have all been criticized but they have all been read and reviewed; some argued that the Church should stay out of politics. Church bodies, from the General Synod to dioceses and parishes, all attracted debate in the media. A government source described *Faith in the City* as 'Marxist theology'; others said that the reports on the family and human relationships did not include enough theology. The report on nuclear warfare was criticized as weakening the United Kingdom during the period of the Cold War. All this thinking was often attacked by the New Right; but to face controversy is one of the Church's tasks in persuading our culture of the gospel's claims. All these reports examined contemporary life and did not confine themselves to life as experienced in the society described in the Old and New Testaments; reality required changes in public policy, not only individual kindness, if justice was to be done.

The underlying question was the most profound of all questions for Christian believers: 'How is God's will to be done?' Those who served on these commissions pointed out how people were actually behaving in schools, families, defence and at work. Those who worshipped, whether occasionally or regularly, agreed that if they accepted the spirit of the story of the Good Samaritan the world must become more humane. They disagreed, of course, on how to do this in a globalized technological society which depends upon responsible, co-operative work.

The divine is not obvious, nor Christian conduct easy to define. Contrasted with God's absolute compassion, our own standards of justice are relative, influenced by our own cultural, psychological and inherited attitudes. How to be a good Samaritan 2000 years after the story was told is complicated for a diplomat, a financier, an economist or a politician, in fact for everyone. If, as the scientists tell us, humanity has 2,000,000,000 years ahead, then we cannot expect the questions to become less complicated.

These questions were frequently argued over at St Paul's Cathedral. After the parable of the Good Samaritan had been read as a lesson at the service of the Order of St Michael and St George, to which many diplomats belong, there was a lively discussion on the practicalities of the Good Samaritan in today's world. Lord Carrington, formerly Foreign Secretary, Lord Gladwyn, formerly Ambassador in Paris and Permanent Representative at the United Nations, and Sir Glyn Jones, immensely experienced in Central Africa, happened to be in a group together, removing the startling robes which members of the Order wear for their ceremony. I put the question: 'What would the Good Samaritan have done if he had arrived while the bandits were actually carrying out the robbery?' One answer was: 'Well, he ought to have sent for the army and shot them up.' Another: 'You can see that the Good Samaritan was a north London social worker. He would have said to the robbers, "I think you need counselling".' Lord Gladwyn remembered days when a rigorous policy might have stopped Hitler; 'We were like a passenger on a sleigh pursued by wolves; it might be a good thing to throw something out for them to eat while we reach for our gun.' What a terrible glimpse of the reality of 1938.

I asked Sir Glyn Jones what was the hardest decision he had ever had to take in the last days of the Empire as a colonial administrator in Africa. He replied: 'When my agricultural advisors discovered that the soil in a whole valley was not able to maintain the population, I had to move hundreds of tribesmen against their will by force, even burning some of their houses. I transported them to a more fertile valley in a relatively unpopulated area.' Asked how they felt about it, now they were self governing, Sir Glyn Jones replied: 'I returned as their guest years after independence. I sat with the leading men and we talked about the old British days. They said to me: "You did right to move us to a more fertile valley; we did not think so at the time but you were right".' In practice, ethical questions may be so complex that it may be decades or even centuries before we can be sure of the decision most in accord with the spirit of the Samaritan. But we have to act immediately.

So there will always be hard decisions which will be criticized. Both *Faith in the City* and *Unemployment and the Future of Work* recommended hard choices. In the words of David Sheppard, then Bishop of Liverpool and one of the Board's chairmen during this time, 'We are saying that there are practical possibilities of bringing about change: this will not be possible without some sacrifice on the part of those who are better off.' David Sheppard himself, since his ordination in 1955, had always chosen to tackle the most demanding tasks, in Canning Town, Woolwich and Liverpool. At the Board there were able Secretaries, Giles Ecclestone, John Gladwin and David Skidmore. They persuaded philosophers, sociologists and theologians to give time to the Board's work. The experienced and committed Church House staff serviced the work and were trusted as equals by Whitehall departments and by voluntary societies.

The contrast between the better off and the deprived was obvious in London, within one mile of St Paul's Cathedral, between, for instance, Brick Lane and the Barbican. In the early eighties London experienced the Brixton riots, and other cities, Manchester, Liverpool, Bristol and Birmingham, had also sent out harsh signals of distress. The City was beginning to boom and to prepare for the Big Bang, when its methods were modernized and changes enabled it to enhance its position as one of the world's top financial centres.

These contrasts challenged St Paul's if it was to be an effective symbol of the gospel especially amongst those whose professional life was in finance. A small group used to meet early in the morning at the Deanery for personal conversation about the duty of committed Christians in the City. Later we arranged meetings either in the Chapter House, or as guests of the *Financial Times*, whose Editor, Richard Lambert, was unfailingly helpful. The group included Sir Richard O'Brien and Patrick Coldstream, the chairmen of the church reports of 1985 and 1997, Andrew Phillips, a City solicitor (now Lord Phillips of Sudbury), and David Arthur, an accountant, and other lay people and clergy. We were concerned that issues of justice and of human rights, what the Bible calls righteousness, should be more openly confronted in our society.

In the autumn of 1985, ten of those interested decided to see for themselves the gap between the prosperous England of the South-East and the neglected England north of the Watford Gap. Could this alleged gulf be bridged? Could St Paul's be a sacrament of concern and support the many voluntary groups working for shared national understanding and prosperity? The group stayed in the Diocesan Conference Centre of Whirlow Grange, Sheffield, founded by Bishop

Leslie Hunter as a place for Christian study and decision making. We included a headteacher, a stockbroker, an accountant and others in business life in London. I myself had been ordained by Dr Hunter in Sheffield in 1942 and met again some of those with whom I had lived and worked as a curate responsible for boys' camps and clubs in the parishes of Attercliffe and Arbourthorne. As I looked back on those years in the blitzed and depressed east end of Sheffield, I realized they were among the most profound experiences of my life.

In Sheffield there was an honourable Christian tradition of social witness, both in the Free Churches and in the Church of England. Leslie Hunter, Bishop from 1939 to 1962, had founded the Sheffield Industrial Mission. He served on the Board for Social Responsibility in London and his vision for the Church of England was of a community for everyone, not narrowly ecclesiastical.

David Arthur, then a partner in the accountancy firm Thomson McLintock, described our feelings of the contrast between Sheffield and the City.

I simply had no idea of the sheer scale of the devastation in the heart of Sheffield. The Lower Don Valley is an area of some four square miles where only a few years ago factories and steel mills clanged and glowed with the activity of thousands of workers. Now hardly any of the works survive. It resembles a great city after the blitz. Vast areas have been razed to the ground. A few of the buildings stand like huge empty cathedrals, their contents sold or scrapped, their work force gone. Shortly, the Tinsley Park steelworks, built in the 1960s as one of the most up-to-date mills in the UK, will join the others, not because of inefficiency or losses, but a victim of the inexorable process of rationalisation of capacity in the steel industry. In 20 years the number of steel workers in the Sheffield area has fallen from 93,000 to 20,000 or below.

At Wath and in Sheffield, we talked to just a few of the unemployed. We learned something of the effects of unemployment on its victims. They told us of the shock of being made redundant with little or no warning after many years' service, the sense of helplessness when application after application is rejected or, more often than not, just received no reply.

The feeling of being cut off when friends and neighbours no
longer want to talk to you ... the further descent into poverty
when after 12 months the unemployment benefit is cut ... the
endless and humiliating battle with officialdom first to discover
what benefit rights exist, and then to avoid the pitfalls that lead
to withdrawal of benefit ... long hours of waiting in DHSS
offices ... finding that nothing can be done because your file is in
another department ... being treated as a scrounger and a suspected cheat, when you would like nothing better than to find a
proper job once more.

A few are lucky enough to find some outlet in voluntary tasks.
One young man, jobless for six years, was cutting the grass in a
churchyard when a DHSS officer came along, armed with his file,
to check up on the work he was doing. A neighbour had 'reported'
him. The tale of misery and humiliation is endless. Individuals
suffer apathy, depression and mental illness. Marriages break down.
Children suffer. Suicides occur.

In December 1985, the Archbishop of Canterbury published the
Report of his Commission on Urban Priority Areas. *Faith in the City*
was a call for action by church and nation, a large volume of 400
pages, the work of a group, lay and ordained. Under the astute
chairmanship of Sir Richard O'Brien, a soldier and industrialist and
former chairman of the Manpower Services Commission, its
recommendations were unanimous. The Archbishop's Commission
undertook visits to cities which had been designated by the Department of the Environment as needing particular assistance. Members
of the Commission visited the dioceses of Liverpool, Newcastle,
Durham and the Stepney area of London, parts of Southwark Diocese,
Birmingham, Lichfield, Coventry and Manchester, receiving direct
evidence and personal impressions from areas in greatest need. The
Report contained many statistics but, to quote its own words,
'Behind the statistics are real people, like the 50-year-old man who
cried when offered a place on a Manpower Services Commission
scheme because he felt wanted again.' The Urban Priority Areas
(UPAs) needed help both from government and from voluntary
bodies.

The Conservative press was critical and its comments appeared to declare a verdict of no confidence. The *Daily Telegraph*, the *Sunday Telegraph* and the *Spectator* were hostile. 'Savourless Salt' was the heading in a leading article which ascribed part of the problems of the inner cities to 'the mass import of people from backward countries to meet an alleged labour shortage'. Though much of the report's evidence came from inner city clergy and lay people living in inner city areas, one comment was that the tone 'conceals an extreme distaste for the life of the poor'. Others suggested that the Church should have condemned the 'sin' and 'wrong doing' of inner city inhabitants. 'Brixton and Tottenham are some contemporary versions of Sodom and Gomorrah.'

Fortunately the *Financial Times*, which had invited a pre-publication briefing at its offices opposite St Paul's, analysed the report, believed that it pointed to soluble problems and even felt it could have been more radical. 'A church not very militant' was its editorial headline. The *Observer* concluded: 'We should be grateful for the Church of England's determination to interpose not only on paper but in the persons of its own clergy and laity more loving responses to poverty and social injustice.' Many clergy from all the churches and vicarage families were reported as suffering from deprivation and even violence. Other commentators felt that a new social conscience was emerging.

The report concluded with 38 recommendations addressed to the Church, 23 to the Government and nation, but none to the business and financial world. We saw our task at St Paul's as making good that omission.

The St Paul's group approached between 200 and 300 men and women working in the City of London, to come to two-hour discussions held in the Chapter House of St Paul's. Our meetings were introduced by Sir Richard O'Brien and by another member of the Archbishop's Commission, David Booth. The facts of the report were generally accepted. The restructuring of industry was causing unfair hardship and the supply of capital was inadequate. Government intervention was required to support the disadvantaged.

I was encouraged to write a considered letter to the Prime Minister to plead for those suffering from unemployment, and as a defence of the Church's concern to be the conscience of the nation. It was intended as a reply to a number of criticisms by government spokesmen, either that the church had no right to concern itself with political matters such as unemployment, or that the Report had been mistaken in the remedies it suggested. Our letter was as follows:

December 1985

Dear Prime Minister

FAITH IN THE CITY

1 We exchanged a few words at the service for Charles Douglas-Home the other week and I thought it might be helpful if I wrote to you briefly.

2 The Church believes that it has itself so far failed to recognise or to respond to the needs of the poor. It has little confidence that, on its present record, it would hear at the last judgment the words of Our Lord to the righteous,

> 'For I was an hungred, and ye gave me meat: I was thirsty, and ye
> gave me drink; I was a stranger, and ye took me in:
> Naked, and ye clothed me: I was sick, and ye visited me: I was in
> prison, and ye came unto me.' (Matthew 25, vv 35 and 36)

3 It confesses this freely: and it intends to do its best to comfort, sustain and enrich those who are the victims of what I believe is an historic sea-change in the character of the western economy, on a par with comparable changes of the past.

4 In this intention, the Church does not make a butt of the Government. Its focus is rather the twin questions of what purposes our democratic society exists to serve; and of how those in work and comparatively well endowed with goods and opportunities can best fulfil the collective obligation towards and provide for those who have no work and who are poorly endowed with goods and opportunities.

5 I doubt whether any of us can see a way through the current economic change or can predict how long it will take for the economy to stabilise itself at a new level of maximum feasible

employment. All that we can see is, I believe, that the change is profound and extensive; that it will probably leave the West with large numbers of long-term unemployed; that we thus face a real risk of establishing a new social 'under' class, with little hope of betterment; and that, more and more, we shall depend on such agencies as the police to bear grievous burdens of stress and anxiety created by the misery and despair of the poor.

6 The Church cannot and does not pretend that it has easy answers. But because the last judgment is the judgment of nations (Matthew 25, v 32), and much more important because Our Lord has no-one but us all to be His ministers to the poor, the Church has a duty to prick the conscience of the nation; and to provoke and join in a debate about the type of society which is being created by economic change and economic policies.

7 Please be assured that my colleagues and I undertake this duty in no partisan spirit, or in the belief that we are holier or better than the Government or any of the Parties. Nor do we believe that throwing money at problems is the right answer. I know that you care for those who suffer. We wish to promote a sense of duty in the nation and its expression in appropriate public action, including appropriate public expenditure. We cannot but believe that this is an aim which you and we have in common.

Alan Webster

We received the following reply:

10 DOWNING STREET

The Prime Minister   15 December 1985

My dear Dean

Thank you for your kind letter following up our conversation at Charles Douglas-Home's memorial service. Your letter raises some serious issues, which are important for government as well as the Church.

I quite understand that the Church feels and, indeed, has a duty to speak to the nation regarding our responsibilities to 'the poor'.

In this respect, it is important that government, just as much as the Church, should never become complacent in the face of need.

I accept your good faith in saying that the Church does not make a butt of government or speak in a partisan spirit. I also very much agree with you that there have been major changes in the character of the Western economy, especially since the oil price increases, which have contributed to the poverty of our inner cities. But there are other factors which the Report could have brought out, including the high concentration of public sector housing, and the lack of choice in education in inner cities, which are surely both important. Similarly, the Report ignores the part played by militantly Left-wing councils, through their refusal to sell derelict land for development, and by their failure to encourage greater enterprise in the private sector. Indeed, in certain cases they seem to go out of their way to discourage enterprise.

We obviously need to do as much as we can to help the inner cities. You emphasise in your letter the care of those who are suffering. This is right, and it is something about which the government is concerned in many of its programmes. But if we go one step further, the government is also concerned to foster wealth-creation in the economy as a whole, to reduce unemployment and to help the poor. In addition, through the sale of council houses, the sale of unused land for development, and other measures directed towards the creation of enterprise, we are trying to create within the inner cities a far less uniform and more flexible economy than exists at present.

I am impressed by the fact that your quotation from the Gospel of Matthew is preceded immediately in the text by the Parable of the Talents. All of us have God-given talents and I believe that it is the responsibility of government to create an environment in which individuals can use their talents to the full.

By arguing almost exclusively in favour of more public spending and a greater role for government through emphasis on collective, rather than individual action, I believe that the Report is in great danger of increasing the helplessness of the very people whom it is trying to help, and of actually discouraging those who wish to help themselves. That cannot be right.

May I say again how grateful I am to you for taking the trouble to write. I do also want to assure you of my continuing great interest and concern with the problems you discuss.

Yours sincerely

Margaret Thatcher

Mrs Thatcher did indeed continue to develop her thinking on religion and society. Three years later, in May 1988, she spoke to the General Assembly of the Church of Scotland. This attracted publicity and, as it was delivered in Edinburgh on the Castle Hill in the hall of the General Assembly, it was nicknamed 'The Sermon on the Mound'. She wittily described in her autobiography *Downing Street Years* spending a Sunday at Chequers working on this with her speech writers, 'down on our knees in an appropriate posture, though drawing on the resources of sellotape, rather than the Holy Spirit'. In this revealing speech 'as a Christian as well as a politician' she emphasized personal responsibility, quoting St Paul: 'If a man will not work he shall not eat'.

Whereas *Faith in the City* had emphasized mutual responsibility within the whole community for the ills of the deprived areas and especially of unemployment, she insisted: 'We are all responsible for our own actions . . . we simply cannot delegate the exercise of mercy and generosity to others.' She admitted she always had difficulty with interpreting the biblical precept to love our neighbours as ourselves, and saw the core of the Christian gospel as one of *choice*. She emphasized three aspects of choice. 'We must choose between good and evil . . . recognize that God works within us in exercising our choice . . . and that Jesus Christ chose to lay down his life.'

The teachings of William Temple on the state's duty to be just and compassionate to all its citizens had not been one of Mrs Thatcher's enthusiasms. She had said that it was because the Good Samaritan had cash that he was remembered and was able to help the man who fell among thieves. She saw in the parable the need for resources if we are to help each other, rather than the challenge to widen our concept of the neighbour.

The previous Prime Minister, Mr Callaghan, discussing this

interpretation of the parable, argued: 'I am astonished at the suggestion that no-one would remember the Good Samaritan if he had not had money. I think of all the kindly voluntary workers in our hospitals . . . They give much of their time and they give themselves. Is that not as worthy a contribution as having money?'

In July 1986 the Mayors of the London Boroughs came to the annual service in St Paul's (nicknamed 'The Chain Gang Service' – their many chains of office might clank during the prayers). But this reflective occasion in the crypt was followed by a reception given by the Lord Mayor of London at Mansion House. The Mayors were of different political parties and of different or no religious convictions, and they worshipped together with goodwill, assured that they accepted each other as public officers committed to serving the citizens who lived in their boroughs.

I had been invited to preach and took my text from the last book of the Bible: 'Behold I make all things new'.

There is so much which is good in our great city. We are right to feel proud of London and of the London Boroughs. But there is much of which we are ashamed; the contrasts are too great. *Lloyds List* recently contained an advertisement for a job for someone between 30 and 40 with a starting salary of £100,000. In shameful contrast is the number of homeless people. Getting ready to start my car after going to a South Bank concert, I found I could not move it because there was a wayfarer sleeping on cardboard in the underground car park beside the car. We know that today there are more than three million unemployed. In the last two or three years there have been serious fires, self-inflicted wounds, in the inner city, Tottenham and Brixton, Toxteth, Handsworth and St Paul's in Bristol. One of our leading bankers, Sir Jeremy Morse, said that 'the state of our inner cities, the urban priority areas, is the most serious problem facing this country.'

During the last year, the Church has done something quite new. It has produced a report, *Faith in the City*, with a large number of recommendations both for its own activities and for society as a whole. The *Financial Times* commented that we have a church which is 'not very militant', but that the analysis contained in the

Report was accurate. About 15% of the population feel that they are alienated, powerless, without work, without good housing. The *Financial Times* argued that '15% is manageable. If we had the social and political and Christian will, the community as a whole could solve this problem.'

Meeting here in St Paul's, near the heart of the city, we all know there is a fundamental difficulty. Our business affairs are determined by the market. Market forces decided that that man or woman at Lloyd's should be paid £100,000 per annum, and no doubt they will, in the language of the market, earn £150,000 a year, or perhaps even £200,000. The question is whether market forces working in this way in the city are really compatible with the presence in these small islands of 15% of the population who do not share this wealth.

The community is reconsidering the proposal that those on Social Security must pay rates. The Bishops of St Albans and Durham, in a House of Lords debate, urged that it was ironical to take away the possibility of work and home ownership, and then stress the need to teach responsibility by enforcing a percentage of rates to be paid. Have market forces become a kind of religious idol? It is impossible for many of our fellow citizens even to find work, let alone own their homes or share the kind of life open to those with very high salaries. God, we know, has a bias to the poor, and this has been classical Christian teaching, but some in the city have annual salaries and benefits in excess of £1,000,000.

Long ago, St Augustine, one of the greatest minds of Europe, wrote his famous book, *The City of God*. He denounced the pagan customs of the late Roman Empire, where the poor fawned on the rich and the rich exploited their dependent clients. He insisted that private alms-giving or church alms-giving are inadequate and urged redistributive taxation. Christ's principles, as in the Sermon on the Mount, are relevant to the happiness and tranquillity of our world.

Pride and envy can haunt very rich individuals. Certainly, the life of the late Paul Getty shows how the demons get to work when wealth is unrestrained. St Augustine was a realist. He called for strong government to assure people of peace. After all, he lived at a time when the frontiers of the Roman Empire were being over-run by the barbarians. But he pointed to an ideal which we must hold high, the ideal proclaimed by Disraeli in the last century: 'Not two nations but one nation'. The ideal was also proclaimed by William Temple when he pleaded for justice after the end of the war. The ideal lurks in the consciences of us all.

In the discussions after the service there was sympathy for the Church. The Mayors knew it was not government policy to encourage major independent social enquiries. Regretting that royal commissions were a thing of the past and that consensus politics were damned as weak, they saw the importance of *Faith in the City*. They knew that its chairman Sir Richard O'Brien had been chairman of the Manpower Services Commission and that the group which wrote the report included Alan Billings, Deputy Leader of Sheffield City Council under David Blunkett.

I was pleading for a change in public opinion to express the need for rebuilding fellowship, human dignity and the whole attitude of the Good Samaritan. Many throughout the country who did not call themselves church people were grateful for the stand which the Church of England took. No institution as pluriform as the Church of England can change rapidly, but inner city congregations and the work of parish priests were respected. The option for the poor was seen to be at the heart of Christianity and conscience to be at the heart of religious faith.

The small *Faith in the City* group continued to meet regularly in the Deanery, early in the day before work, chaired by Sir Richard. Our secretary, David Arthur, had by now become Secretary of the Industrial Christian Fellowship and volunteered to give part-time service on the administrative side for a year. Visits were paid to Walsall in the Midlands at the invitation of the municipal authorities, the churches and the Chamber of Trade, where plans were being made to strengthen existing job creation schemes – an unusual combination of municipal co-operation, private capital and work by the churches, which was growing in the Urban Priority Areas.

We saw our objectives as changing attitudes and gaining acceptance for the idea that it is right for companies, while pursuing the essential objectives of profit, service and efficiency, to accept a wider responsibility to society, and particularly towards the Urban Priority Areas.

We intended to do this by promoting discussion, particularly at senior levels; by trying to find out about activities which some companies were already undertaking in acceptance of such wider responsibilities (e.g. Business in the Community, Project Fullemploy, and others); by helping to draw attention to these; and by encouraging other companies to follow these examples.

Other related topics, such as 'probity', business ethics and codes of practice, tended to become entwined with the main issue of social responsibility and inter-dependence, although this was not our original intention.

We saw the need for an additional message to City firms (and financial institutions with head offices elsewhere), to accept wider responsibilities for themselves. They should make clear to the industrial and commercial companies in which they invest, and which they advise, that the acceptance of wider responsibilities is not only acceptable as part of their overall objectives, but also desirable.

These activities might include lending money to businesses or projects in the UPAs, which involved an above-average risk, without imposing above-average terms and conditions. One of the complaints received from UPAs was that it was very difficult to obtain finance at all for valuable job-creating projects. Contrary to continental practice (e.g. in Germany) investors were looking for quick payback, and the pressure of performance ratings caused fund managers to press companies for good short-term results, to the detriment of the longer term. How could counter-pressures be created?

After a year's negotiation the Governor of the Bank of England hosted a mid-day meeting at the Bank for 70 industrialists and financial leaders, on 27 January 1987, at which the Archbishop of Canterbury spoke and answered questions. Copies of his speech were widely circulated. We gained access to the gilded halls of the Bank, thanks to the support of Peter Brooke, MP for the City and Westminster, and a consistent friend of St Paul's. Some of the Bank staff hesitated over this meeting on the grounds that the report was 'political' and a 'piece of social engineering'. The Archbishop appealed for partnership at all levels, for the spirit of 'can do', which he found in the City of London; he sensed its need in the Urban Priority Areas also. He questioned negative attitudes. 'I recently read of a successful American business man who said "Greed is all right . . . You can be greedy and still feel good about yourself."' (His name was Ivan Boesky, a New York financier, and he had recently been jailed for fraud.) The Archbishop then said:

> The report warns that frustration, lack of hope and a sense of powerlessness form an inflammable mixture that can be ignited all too easily. There is a real danger of a growing perception that the only way to obtain change is to opt out of the unwritten rules and relationships that maintain our social fabric, and succumb instead to the forces of unreason and despair (Fortress Wapping and Tottenham riots).
>
> Such a condition runs directly contrary to everything that the Church stands for, and must exercise everybody whose principles and interests require concern for the state of society and for our fellow citizens. I take it as axiomatic that this must include the City of London, and the fact of this meeting confirms my view. I also take it as axiomatic that any response to the situation the report describes needs the contribution of business and finance if it is to succeed.
>
> But I must not talk solely in apocalyptic terms – to do so would be inadequate for a Christian and untrue to *Faith in the City*. The report found signs of hope in urban priority areas, and willingness to build on them. The Bible ends with a vision of a new city and that encourages us to think of what might be. I share this vision.
>
> We need to ask 'Whose responsibility are our urban priority areas?' To answer that they are simply the Government's is insufficient. The record of central and local government here may be ambiguous, but we have no right to criticise if our own stance is simply 'leave it to them'. As a Christian, I believe the answer to my question is that these areas are the responsibility of all of us. As a realist, I believe that solutions built on partnership between different interests are more likely to succeed. It seems to me that

many different kinds of resources are called for if our cities are to be won back from what some of them are today, many different kinds of venture and initiative, many different kinds of talent and innovation – working in harmony – the financier and the architect, the businessman and the philanthropist, the legislator and the planner, the police and social worker, the churchman and the educationalist, the landscape artist and civil engineer.

I claim that the resources, the political will, the public support and the practical policies are either there or potentially there, provided we as a nation have a vision of common citizenship to inspire us. Unless there is that collective commitment to one nation, then the fears, tensions and bitterness will fester and amplify. There really is no choice. In the past we've united against various real or imagined enemies without, often to very good effect. I believe we now have to recognise the enemy within which is frankly a lack of moral cohesion. The miseries and deprivations in the inner city are not other people's problems. They are our problems.

It is the wealth that is created here and in similar places that is going to be needed.

In the following months the Archbishop, at the group's suggestion, wrote to the Chairmen of 200 City firms, inviting them to discuss with their boards two questions:

First, it is not suggested that companies generally are concerned only with maximising profits: for example they accept a responsibility to their customers and employees as well as to their shareholders. But there is also the question of whether non-commercial initiatives should be left to the government and private citizens.

Secondly, what greater responsibility could your company accept towards people in the urban priority areas?

Although the Archbishop asked the Chairmen to let him know the outcome of their discussions, less than one in three did in fact reply. Out of those, some were warm and supportive, some were negative, and the majority fairly lukewarm and non-committal. 'We are already working through Business in the Community, and we are unlikely to be able to do much more' was a fairly typical response. And indeed, by 1986, some 300 companies were signed-up members of BIC, and many valuable projects were being supported.

It was encouraging to hear, from other parts of the UK, how companies and institutions could enter into partnerships with local people, public bodies and voluntary organizations, to promote job-creating projects and to provide training for people out of work. The Steering Group had become involved with one particular project, in Walsall, and spent some time helping the local people to get it organized. A number of members had visited Walsall in support, but it soon became clear that the Group did not have the resources to undertake that kind of activity on an ongoing basis.

An official of the Bank of Boston wrote from Massachusetts – a letter typical of those who grasped the core message of *Faith in the City*:

I have had the opportunity to read carefully the Archbishop's remarks. I found them to be very relevant to our experience particularly as it concerns the issue of opportunities for minorities in declining inner cities.

As you are undoubtedly aware, American cities are also developing two distinct classes – one which has benefited from the growth in the American economy and one which has been left behind. It is a matter of great concern to us that growth in the latter category is accelerating.

We share your belief that the private sector can have a strong role in helping to revitalize disadvantaged urban areas and it is in this context that the Council for Economic Action, a non-profit organization that I chair, created the Small Business Development System. At the very heart of this program is the belief that the most direct means through which those who have been left behind can be integrated into our society is through economic enfranchisement resulting from business ownership.

At this time we are operating the SBDS in twelve urban areas throughout the United States. And while the output of the SBDS is just beginning to come on stream, over 1,300 potential business managers have been trained and over 100 new businesses have been created by June of 1987. The majority of these new business enterprises are owned by minorities and are in troubled neighbourhoods. By the end of this year, we project that an additional 1,000 business managers will be trained and an additional 150 new business enterprises will be started.

Today there are changed attitudes in many companies. The RSA 'Tomorrow's Company' project; the work of the Institute of Business Ethics; the general recognition that widespread unemployment and poverty is 'bad for business' and that the spending of company funds on inner city projects can be justified by long-term profit criteria, are all evidence of the seeds of new thinking.

The Church Urban Fund raised £37 million from church people throughout the country and enabled nearly 3,000 projects in community work. It has provided the seed-corn for inner city projects, attracting additional funds from government, local and charitable sources. One of the most remarkable church-inspired projects was around the Anglican cathedral at Liverpool where Dean Derrick Walters' Operation Primrose raised over £200 million in loans and grants for imaginative urban renewal including a hospital, a factory and university buildings as well as new housing.

In many parts of the country, dioceses and local teams produced their own 'Faith in the City' reports, as the basis for local action to tackle unemployment, homelessness and poverty. Partnerships were set up. The launch of the Herts and Beds Church & Industry Partnership was chaired by David Arthur.

Many charities and pressure groups joined in: Church Action with the Unemployed, Church Action on Poverty, New Economics Foundation, Basic Income Research Group and Child Poverty Action Group all gave strong leads. They supported individuals and families in distress, badgering the government for action and generating new ideas, such as credit unions, self-build housing schemes and local economic trading schemes and putting them into practice.

Mrs Thatcher's government also got on with the job of tackling inner city deprivation. There is some evidence that the *Faith in the City* report did sting others into action, and led to an earlier and greater involvement and commitment than might otherwise have been the case. Perhaps too the change of government after the 1997 election and the promises to listen to what the public and the churches were saying suggest that the appeals to conscience were not wasted.

The Church of England's Church Urban Fund has enabled many initiatives by inner city parishes in depressed areas, which would have been impossible without it. Public attitudes towards unemployment became more humane and much greater efforts were made to enable the disadvantaged to find jobs. Of course the recovery in the economy was crucial but meanwhile central government, local authorities, trade unions, companies, and voluntary bodies learnt to co-operate. The country, the Church, individual firms, cities and local authorities focused on the harsh problem of unemployment. Part of the motivation has been the teaching of Christianity, felt and obeyed rather than openly acknowledged.

> What doth the Lord require of thee,
> but to do justly, and to love mercy,
> and to walk humbly with thy God?
> (Micah 6.8, AV)

References

Archbishop of Canterbury's Commission on Urban Priority Areas, *Faith in the City: a Call for Action by Church and Nation*. London, Church House Publishing, 1985.

Booth-Clibborn, Stanley, *Taxes – Burden or Blessing?* Berkhamsted, Arthur James, 1991.

Clark, Henry, *The Church under Thatcher*. London, SPCK, 1993.

Evans, Christopher, *St Luke*. London, SCM Press, 1990.

Raban, Jonathan, *God, Man and Mrs Thatcher*. London, Chatto and Windus, 1989.

Selby, Peter, *Grace and Mortgage*. London, Darton, Longman & Todd, 1997.

Sheppard, David, *Bias to the Poor*. London, Hodder and Stoughton, 1983.

6 THE FALKLANDS SERVICE: Reconciliation after War

Cathedrals and churches remind us of the living God in the societies where they are set. In the words of Dean Inge:

> It is a vision of timeless reality which is neither born nor dies, being raised above the changes and chances of this mortal life. We pray God that we who are careful and troubled about many things may repose upon his eternal changelessness. We attempt to realise, in thought and feeling, the immanence of the temporal in the eternal, and of the eternal in the temporal; a spiritual religion, based on a firm belief in absolute and eternal values – an entirely open mind towards the discoveries of science, a reverent and receptive attitude towards the beauty, sublimity and wisdom of the creation.

1981 and 1982 were pressurized years at St Paul's Cathedral. The media glamour of the royal wedding in July 1981 made great demands on the staff but increased mutual trust; the tragedies of the marriage were hidden in the future. The splendours and the moving moments of this service were seen round the world by 800 million people. Worshippers and visitors from Britain and abroad afterwards poured into the building. Some were questioning and searching for faith, quietly praying both in the cathedral and below in the crypt. As admission was free, the cathedral also had troubled droppers-in: a trial at the Old Bailey might bring the families of the accused; relations of patients at St Bartholomew's came to St Paul's for rest and prayer; there were always homeless people at the back of the nave. One, nicknamed Black Jack, who spent much of the day

sitting on a radiator, was well known to virgers and Friends. Sister
Hilary of the Wantage Community, chaplains, virgers and Friends
were available for conversation and help. All this against a background of other creative work: school parties had to be looked after,
while people crowded in to the lectures and poetry readings organized by Canon Pilkington, as well as to the many musical occasions
under the direction of Christopher Dearnley.

On 2 April 1982, to the fury and astonishment of the British
Government, the Falkland Islands were occupied by Argentinian
forces. It was so unexpected; some British officials had hoped that
over 25 years a generation of young Falklanders might grow up who
had their secondary education in Argentina and possibly married
Argentinians. Lord Carrington, the Foreign Secretary, had joked in
the early 1980s that the Islands were foreign policy priority number
242 for Her Majesty's Government. It had been announced that the
only British naval presence, HMS *Endurance*, was to be withdrawn
from the Falklands and South Georgia. Negotiations were dragging
on through the United Nations; Sir Nicholas Ridley, a Foreign
Office minister, had visited the Islands. But the Islanders, supported
by back-bench MPs, had blocked concessions to Argentina. Lord
Carrington had failed to take steps to prevent, or respond to, the
Argentinian invasion, and resigned on 5 April speaking of 'a
national humiliation'.

After the invasion the Task Force was despatched, but negotiations
continued until the first lives were lost when a British nuclear sub-
marine sank the cruiser *Belgrano* on 2 May with the loss of over 300
Argentinian lives; the Argentinian air force retaliated by sinking
HMS *Sheffield* two days later. On 12 June the final attack on Port
Stanley began and the surrender document was signed on 14 June.
About 1,000 were killed in the fighting, 253 British and the rest
Argentinian. The British Government asked St Paul's Cathedral to
hold a thanksgiving service. Then, to quote the World Council of
Churches: 'the disagreement between State and Church developed
and raised profound theological issues . . . Is our God a tribal deity
whose dominion coincides with what remains of the British
Empire, or is he the Lord of heaven and earth to whom all nations
owe allegiance?'

It was agreed that the service must be ecumenical. We wished to affirm the courage and success of the Task Force, share the grief of the mourners and acknowledge that wars are a sign of failure rather than triumph. During June and July a public debate raged about the service and an avalanche of letters descended on Lambeth Palace, the Methodist leader Kenneth Greet, Cardinal Hume and St Paul's Cathedral. The Pope visited England in June, was welcomed by massive crowds, and in Coventry, which had suffered such devastation in World War II, made a heartfelt cry for peace. 'Today, the scale and the horror of modern warfare, whether nuclear or not, makes it totally unacceptable as a means of settling differences between nations.'

St Paul's had long been associated with British wars. Here were buried Nelson, Wellington and Jellicoe. It was occasionally described as the 'National Valhalla', the hall in which, in Scandinavian mythology, slain heroes feasted. In 1915 the Bishop of London had led 3,000 Territorials from Trafalgar Square to an altar built of drums on the west steps. His sermon was printed as the message of 'The Bishop of the Battlefields'. A London vicar, who spent time as an army chaplain, wrote: 'Every shot that is fired . . . is in very truth for His name's sake.' The Dardanelles expedition was 'a new crusade'.

But poets protested. Kipling's 'Recessional', often associated with St Paul's and its grand services, began:

> God of our fathers, known of old
> Lord of our far flung battle line . . .

but went on to foresee a changed world after the end of Empire:

> The tumult and the shouting dies
> The Captains and the Kings depart

and described as 'heathen' the heart that put its trust

> In reeking tube and iron shard.

Wilfred Owen, who won the MC in World War I and died as a gallant and effective officer, wrote to his mother:

Christians have deliberately *cut* some of the main teachings of their code . . . I saw God through mud.

Preparations for Prayer

Increasingly the ambiguities and tragedies of war undermined the patriotic simplicities of singing 'Onward Christian Soldiers' or speaking of 'Holy Wars'. The traumas of modern war made a triumphalistic 'Victory Service' a contradiction in terms. Both the Deanery and Lambeth Palace received a vast correspondence. Amongst the first letters to arrive was one written by a theologian who had served in World War II.

The Service will verge on blasphemy and certainly deeply threaten the capacity of the Church for any effective mission and witness if it simply blesses the whole episode and echoes the mood of euphoria and imperialistic nostalgia which has been evoked in some quarters. There must be a strong note of prayer and penitence which, while it includes real praise and thanksgiving for heroism, service and efficiency in carrying out a task assigned, recognizes that that task should never have become necessary and the fact of it being found necessary, or thought to be so, is the result of grievous errors on our side as well as elsewhere.

National self-respect requires constant attention to building up the community within the nation. The crisis of our inner-cities, for example, is far more serious than would have been the 'loss' of the Falklands and has far greater implications for our future welfare and our capacity to contribute to the peace of the world. Where is the money and the 'task-force' approach for this?

I am frightened by our current fantasy and jingoism.

A correspondent in London wrote:

Nationalism cannot override Christianity; it has been so tragic that in this war, as in so many others over the centuries, soldiers of both nations have believed that God is on the side of their government's political claims. I happen to have been brought up a Protestant, but I welcome the respect for the Catholic Church which quoting the Pope's own words would demonstrate. Since Argentina is Catholic, I hope too it would show how our shared Christian beliefs can transcend political differences.

Just as the Geneva Convention allows us to treat any wounded man as a human being rather than as an enemy, so it seems to me a sensitive extension of this concession to 'permit' our sympathy for the bereaved of both sides, and also our respect for any soldier who sacrifices his life for his country's cause, even when it is opposed to ours.

I have heard only one first-hand story from a plain soldier in the task force. It isn't concerned with heroism, but it touches the heart. This British soldier was detailed to check a group of Argentine prisoners, in case they were still holding weapons. One Argentinian had a sack, which he begged the British not to make him open, but he had to obey orders. In the sack were the mangled remains of the Argentinian's 16-year-old brother, which he was trying to take home to his mother. It was not allowed. The British boy is suffering from exposure and frostbite – and I think a pain in his heart. How can one keep pity for any one and not the others, these poor young men involved in massacre instead of glory?

I am shocked that a Prime Minister should have any say in how a church service should be. This is not a time for Union Jacks and saluting guns, but for prayer and sorrow, and hope that out of the horror and sorrow can come a wider, truer desire for peace – not victory.

Many wrote to urge integrity at St Paul's:

We heard on the radio this morning that you are trying to ensure that the Falklands Service in the Cathedral is not a celebration of triumphant chauvinism and militarism. You will be much criticised and even vilified. We want you to know that we and many, many others hope that you will carry through your intentions for this service. The issues at stake are so important, being nothing less than the integrity of the Gospel and the catholicity of the Church, that you and the Chapter must not give way to the forces which would make Christianity merely the sanctification of chauvinism.

Other letters took a different line:

> We believe that it is wrong to steal. The military occupation of territory outside a nation's boundary is armed robbery on a large scale. I have seen no convincing case made out for the United Kingdom not having sovereignty over the Falklands Islands: it is certain that Argentina has no right to them. Surely then we should rejoice at the liberation of territory from alien control.
>
> It seems there is a pacifist taking a prominent part in the service. He, and all of us, have our freedoms – *including freedom of worship* – because people have fought for our freedom: particularly against Hitler and National Socialism. We were alone in Europe in 1940 against him and his staunch ally Stalin. It appears to be wholly wrong therefore to have pacifists included in the service.
>
> There is to me a deeper reason. If we do not clearly say that occupation of another nation's territory is wrong, then the people of Cambodia, Afghanistan, Latvia and so on may be induced to think that they will not have their own administration restored, and we are not endeavouring to restore religious freedom to them.

In the daily stream of letters there were many contrasting opinions:

> As a member of the Church of England, I ask you to cancel the proposed Service of Thanksgiving in connection with the Falklands Islands.

and

> Such a service is so widely open to mis-interpretation that it can only do harm to the image of the Churches and cause untold grief to the survivors on all sides.

and

> One reads in 'The Daily Telegraph' – a paper a lot less sensational than most – that considerable discussion has taken place as to the form of the service re the Falklands tragedy which is to be held. I do trust, Sir, that you will do your duty and not allow it to be

turned into a circus. Further, I cannot but feel it would be very proper if the Lord's Prayer were said in Spanish. But above all I do trust that you will do your duty and pray for the souls of all Argentinians and British alike.

and

I am writing, as a life-long Anglican and a patriot, to ask you, respectfully, NOT to allow the Lord's Prayer to be said in Spanish at the Falklands Thanksgiving Service which is to be held in St Paul's. Also, considering the views of Dr K Greet on the Falklands campaign, I beg you not to ask him to take part in the service.

The problems of conscience faced by pacifists during the Falklands conflict were severe. The Argentinian invasion in April was ordered by a brutal government, the immediate decision of the British Government to send the Task Force received the almost unanimous approval of Parliament at a brief Saturday emergency session, and General Galtieri had such an evil record of political assassinations and 'disappearances' that public opinion inside and outside the churches was almost united in favour of the use of force if negotiations at the United Nations failed to turn back the invasion.

Not for the first time in the British religious tradition, it was Nonconformists who asked the hard questions. One of the most courageous pacifists, prepared to oppose British policy even while the Task Force was on its way south in April and May, was Dr Kenneth Greet, a leading Methodist minister and in 1982 Moderator of the Free Church Federal Council which represents Presbyterians, Baptists and Congregationalists as well as his own Methodist Church. Throughout the conflict he appeared on platforms and on TV advocating negotiation and was prepared to challenge British policy even while the members of the forces were dying in the fighting needed to remove the 10,000 Argentinians from the Islands. Such a radical and prominent opponent of the Government's policy was strongly condemned as unpatriotic even by some fellow Methodists. But he stood firm.

Pax Christi, Peace and Justice groups, the Quakers and various Christian Pacifist organizations also spoke out against a military solution. Strict pacifists were joined by members of the United Nations Association and by some members of the Labour Party, notably Tam Dalyell MP. Tam Dalyell believed that the Government had not been sincerely committed to negotiation and that the sinking of the *Belgrano* on 2 May was intended to end negotiations, even though it was known in Washington and London that the *Belgrano* and its escorts were returning to the mainland. A small minority in Britain felt on grounds of principle and of political wisdom that we ought to be negotiating and not fighting.

Ought those who had taken a pacifist line take part in the service? Some pacifist groups, especially the Pax Christi group in central London, whose sponsors were two bishops (the Anglican, Mark Santer, and the Roman Catholic, David Konstant), considered holding an independent service in protest at what they feared would be a jingoistic event at St Paul's. Twenty members of various pacifist groups came to the Deanery to explain their views and fears. Some of their members had spoken of a protest on the steps of St Paul's, some of a service in Hyde Park, some Roman Catholics of simply holding a Requiem Mass for the Fallen. I felt that it was the duty of the Church of England to enable us all to pray and witness together and persuaded them that the service would not offend their principles.

The churches' planning group met at the Deanery on 30 June. The seventeen members were aware of the main requests coming from the public through correspondence and the newspapers. This was the first time a national service had received such a torrent of advice. The bodies represented included the Dean and Chapter and musicians of St Paul's, the Ministry of Defence, the Palace, the Church of Scotland, the Free Churches, the Roman Catholic Church and Kneller Hall acting for all the military musicians. The need to be sensitive to the feelings of the mourners led us to rule out invitations to Argentinians, or to saying the Lord's Prayer in Spanish, even though it had been said in Spanish in Coventry after the loss of HMS *Coventry*. We were anxious that it should not be a military service with swords and guards of honour or parts of the liturgy taken by military leaders. The shape of the service – thanksgiving, remembrance and reconciliation – was decided at this meeting, and we agreed to remain in touch with each other.

Many comments came from Parliament in questions or motions, not all of which reached the pages of Hansard. The earliest attracted many signatories including Alan Clark, Viscount Cranbourn, Sir Bernard Braine, Anthony Beaumont Dark and Julian Amery:

> This House calls on the Dean and Chapter of St Paul's to ensure that the Order of Service in the Cathedral on July 26 includes prayers of thanksgiving for the victory of British Arms in the South Atlantic and the liberation of the Falkland Islands from foreign domination.

This was followed on 20 July with an oral exchange between Sir Bernard Braine and the Prime Minister, the day overshadowed by serious IRA bomb explosions with loss of life in London.

Sir Bernard Braine: Have the organisers of next Monday's service at St Paul's Cathedral said to my Right Hon. Friend whether prayers will be offered for the earlier victims of the junta – many thousands of whom included British subjects – and whether the prayers will be for the early release of such people, or at least for some identification of where the bodies of the dead lie?

The Prime Minister: I do not believe that that will come into the service – (Hon Members: 'Why not?') Because it is a service of thanksgiving for the liberation of the Falkland Islands, and of remembrance of the fallen. During that service we shall remember all the fallen and all of those who have given their lives so that freedom and justice might continue.

Two days later, during the crisis in London caused by the IRA and fears in the country from rising unemployment, there were more written questions and answers.

Viscount Cranbourn asked the Prime Minister whether consultations have taken place between the Government and the Dean of St Paul's about the form of service in the cathedral on 26 July.

The Prime Minister: The form of service in St Paul's cathedral is the responsibility of the Dean and Chapter, but we have passed on to the Dean our views on how to make this a national occasion.

Sir John Biggs-Davison asked the Prime Minister what arrangements have been made for the representation of the Armed Forces of the Crown, and relations, at the Falklands Islands service in St Paul's Cathedral; and whether uniform will be worn and colours paraded.

The Prime Minister: The Armed Forces will be represented at the Falkland Islands Service by a large contingent from the Task Force, as well as by senior officers, including the chiefs of staff and senior operational commanders. The next of kin of those who fell in the operations have been invited to attend. Members of the Armed Forces at the service will be in uniform. I understand that colours will not be paraded.

Ideas about the service continued to pour in from members of the churches, and the general public. It was fortunate that all the churches were acting together as some politicians were suggesting that the Church of England, as a 'state church', was in duty bound to confine itself to the advice of the Government. Some pointed out that the Archbishop of Canterbury and the majority of the Chapter of St Paul's were crown appointments and should remember the Establishment. With the support of the other churches the Church of England did not compromise and this enabled the Archbishop of Canterbury in his courageous sermon to represent the consensus of thinking within the churches, as well as the majority of the country outside them. Cardinal Hume wrote afterwards: 'I was only sorry he got all the criticism and we hid behind him.'

The Cabinet, especially William Whitelaw, was interested in the evolving service as the details were worked out. Sir Arthur Hockaday, Under Secretary of State in the Ministry of Defence, came to St

Paul's to take note of what was being decided. We agreed that we might be able to help and unite the nation, the forces, the bereaved, and do a little to prepare for reconciliation with Argentina – a country which had a long history of friendship and trade with the UK and large English and Welsh communities who had lived at peace with their neighbours during the conflict.

A Service to Remember

Early on the morning of 26 July there were already crowds round St Paul's. I walked from the Deanery past *Daily Mail* posters advertising 'Why I would not go to St Paul's today', an article arguing that the service was designed to insult the Queen, the Prime Minister and the mourners, and was 'a service of revenge by the clerical establishment'. Some mourners, already in their seats after the long journey from South Wales, were quietly weeping. I sat with them and we prayed together; being alongside seemed best. We looked at the hymns and prayers in the Order of Service together.

In another part of the cathedral were wives and widows from Portsmouth. The Order of Service in their hands requested members of the congregation to stand as processions entered. A journalist told me: 'The relatives were not at all happy. They had refused to stand up for the Government or Margaret Thatcher or any of that lot (I expect that included the clergy). They blamed them for the needless loss of their menfolk. They had decided they would only stand up for the Queen, who entered last. A much beribboned senior army officer came over while those interminable processions were entering, and demanded to know who was in charge of "these people" – with a contemptuous wave of the hand – and why did they not make them stand up. The petty officer replied "We are in charge. They are naval widows, sir. *You* make them!" The officer went away muttering, tail between legs. It gave the POs much satisfaction.'

The many processions of clergy, the Lord Mayor, the various members of the Royal Family took twenty minutes until all were in their places – the Queen and the Royal Family, the Prime Minister and Mr Thatcher, John Nott, the Minister of Defence and Francis Pym, the new Foreign Secretary. The Cabinet, the Opposition and

Members of Parliament were on the south side of the dome, the military commanders on the north side. The service was televised and broadcast throughout the world, including Argentina. The congregation of 2,500 first sang the thanksgiving hymn 'Praise my soul the King of Heaven'. Before the Chaplain of the Fleet led us in the General Thanksgiving, I went to the pulpit to speak the words of the Bidding Prayer hoping to unite the many points of view of those sharing the service in the Cathedral, the streets outside and, through the media, in the UK and for some around the world.

> We meet to worship God. We thank Him for the cessation of hostilities in the South Atlantic and for the courage, determination and endurance of those who took part, and for the safe return of so many.
>
> We remember the fallen and commend them to God's keeping. May He work in them the good purpose of His perfect will. We pray for the wounded and all who care for them. We seek to share the sufferings of those who mourn, and pray that God may strengthen them now and in the years ahead.
>
> We pray for reconstruction in the Falkland Islands and for the reunion of divided families. We pray for peace and reconciliation in the South Atlantic. Let this service unite us, strengthen our spirit and sustain our hopes so that we commit ourselves to be makers of peace in a divided world.

After a hymn by Robert Bridges, 'All my hope on God is founded', the first lesson was read by Mrs Rosalind Goodfellow, Moderator of the United Reformed Church. She was the only woman to speak during the service, though the TV cameras frequently noticed the black-clad women mourners, sometimes tearful, sometimes holding children. The words of the lesson from Micah 4 included the universal human vision of a warless world, tragically so far away:

> They shall beat their swords into ploughshares,
> and their spears into pruning hooks;
> nation shall not lift up sword against nation,
> neither shall they learn war any more;

but they shall sit every man under his vine and under his fig tree, and none shall make them afraid.
(Micah 4.3–4, RSV)

The second theme in the service, Remembrance, opened with a member of the Task Force standing at the choir rails, saying in the determined voice of a soldier: 'Remember before God those who died in the conflict. The eternal God is thy refuge, and underneath are the everlasting arms.' After a Wesley hymn, 'Let saints on earth . . .', David Cooper, Chaplain of the Second Battalion the Parachute Regiment, involved in the bitterest fighting at Mount Longdon, read the Beatitudes. The choir sang an anthem which included the words of the promise 'God shall wipe away all tears from their eyes and there shall be no more death', and the Archbishop preached. He himself had won the Military Cross in the Second World War for rescuing a comrade from a blazing tank.

The first note in this service is thanksgiving . . . What I have heard about the conduct of the British forces in and around the Falkland Islands has moved and heartened me. I have experienced battle myself and know that it is no mean achievement to preserve the restraint and display the courage shown by so many of those involved in this conflict . . . At the hard fought battle of Goose Green the reaction was not the conquerors' triumph, but 'thank God it's stopped'. It is right to be proud of such men. There is much to give thanks for in all this now that the attempt to settle the future of the Falkland Islanders by armed invasion has been thwarted . . . While giving thanks, however, we also mourn for grievous losses. Thank God so many returned, but there are many in this cathedral who mourn the loss of someone they love and our hearts go out to them.

We possess the terrifying power for destruction. War has always been detestable, but since 1945 we have lived with the capacity to destroy the whole of humankind. It is impossible to be a Christian and not to long for peace. 'Blessed are the peacemakers for they shall be called the Sons of God.' This was one of the themes to which the Pope repeatedly returned during his visit to this country. His speech in Coventry was particularly memorable when he said 'war should belong to the tragic past, to history. It should find no place on humanity's agenda for the future.'

Our hope as Christians is not fundamentally in man's naked goodwill and rationality. We believe that he can overcome the deadly selfishness of class or sect or race by discovering himself as a child of the universal God of love. When a man realizes that he is a beloved child of the creator of all, then he is ready to see his neighbours in the world as brothers and sisters . . . Those who dare to interpret God's will must never claim him as an asset for one nation or group rather than another. War springs from the love and loyalty which should be offered to God, being applied to some God substitute, one of the most dangerous being nationalism.

This is a dangerous world where evil is at work nourishing the mindless brutality which killed and maimed so many in this city last week. Sometimes with the greatest reluctance force is necessary in order to hold back the chaos which injustice and the irrational element in man threaten to make of the world. But all is not lost and there is hope. Even in the failure of war there are springs of hope. In that great war play by Shakespeare, Henry V says 'there is some soul of goodness in things evil, would men observingly distil it out'.

People are mourning on both sides of this conflict. In our prayers we shall quite rightly remember those who are bereaved in our own country and the relations of the young Argentinian soldiers who were killed. Common sorrow could do something to re-unite those who were engaged in this struggle. A shared anguish can be a bridge of reconciliation. Our neighbours are indeed like us.

God is able to work upon us. He is able to deepen and enlarge our compassion and to purify our thanksgiving. The parent who comes mourning the loss of a son may find here consolation, but also a spirit which enlarges our compassion to include all those Argentinian parents who have lost sons.

Man without God finds it difficult to achieve this revolution inside himself. But talk of peace and reconciliation is just fanciful and theoretical unless we are prepared to undergo such a revolution. Many of the reports I have heard about the troops engaged in this war refer to moments when soldiers have been brought face to face with what is fundamental in life and have found new sources of strength and compassion even in the midst of conflict. Ironically, it is sometimes those people who remained at home, whether supporters or opponents of the conflict, who continue to be most belligerent in their attitudes and untouched in their deepest selves.

Cathedrals and churches are always places into which we bring human experiences – birth, marriage, death, our flickering communion with God, our fragile relationships with each other, so that they may be deepened and directed by the spirit of Christ. Today we bring our mixture of thanksgiving, sorrows and aspirations for a better ordering of this world.

Pray God that he may purify, enlarge and redirect these in the ways of his kingdom of love and peace. Amen.

The Archbishop's wise and courageous sermon summed up the themes of the whole service and gave definition to national reflection on the Falklands conflict. The theme of Remembrance continued with prayers written by the Moderator of the Church of Scotland, Dr John McIntyre, and by Cardinal Basil Hume, Archbishop of Westminster.

For the Wounded, led by John McIntyre:

O Christ, our Master and Redeemer, you were wounded for the salvation of all mankind, your body broken for the peace of the world. Hear us, therefore, as we now commend to your loving care all who have been wounded in body, mind or spirit in recent conflict: the blind, the maimed and disabled, the mentally distraught, all for whom life will never now be the same. Grant them healing of body and mind, strengthening of spirit and confidence, and whatever the future holds for them, the encouragement of good companionship and of understanding love, for your dear sake. Amen.

For Remembrance, led by Basil Hume:

Lord our God, you guide your creation with fatherly care. Your will is to gather all peoples as one family in yourself. Banish violence from our midst and wipe away our tears, so that we may not only be called your sons and daughters, but live as true brothers and sisters in Christ your son.

God our Father, in whom the dead find life, listen we beseech you to our prayers. Grant that all who have fallen in battle may find in you the peace that this world cannot give, and enjoy eternal life.

God our Father, you know how saddened we are by the death of those for whom our love is great. We ask you to comfort and console those who mourn and grieve. We make our prayer through Christ our Lord. Amen.

It was noticed how personal and intimate were the Cardinal's prayers and how the Moderator prayed for all who were wounded and remembered the mental traumas now known to be so devastating after armed conflict.

These prayers, said from the choir screen for the wounded and the fallen, faded into silence. Two trumpeters now stood, brilliantly lit, on the gallery of Christopher Wren's majestic dome, high above the congregation, for the haunting notes of the Last Post. The two minutes' silence which followed was made even more poignant by a child crying in its mother's arms among the mourners in the echoing nave.

Thoughts in the silence turned to those lost in all wars. I remembered a cousin, a chaplain to the Paratroopers, killed in his parachute at the crossing of the Rhine at the end of World War II. *The Times'* religious correspondent, Clifford Longley, below the pulpit with other journalists, realized that he might have been with the mourners, had his son, a sailor in the Task Force, not returned safely. The silence was long, not serene, but weighed down with anguish that so many have had lives cut short by war. 'The pity of war' could be felt in the cathedral. The television watchers round the world saw a lighted candle burning on the high altar. Then Reveille came from above our heads and we were released again into our own lives; a member of the Task Force repeated the words 'Let not your hearts be troubled, neither let them be afraid'. He recalled us to the work of building peace and working for reconciliation, the final theme of the service.

It was a relief to sing the 23rd Psalm, 'The Lord's my Shepherd', to the tune Crimond, with unusual fervour, especially the verse:

> My table thou hast furnished
> In presence of my foes;
> My head thou dost with oil anoint
> And my cup overflows.

Canon Douglas Webster, the Canon in Residence, read the third lesson which included the advice 'Do not let the sun go down upon your anger' (Ephesians 4.25–end). The Bishop of London led us in the confession and the absolution, the confession intended to include the failure of the nations and not only personal sins. Kenneth Greet, the pacifist whose inclusion in the service had caused so much controversy, led us in prayer with his moving image of the rainbow:

> Eternal God, as the rainbow spans the heavens when the clouds are dark, so our strifes and enmities stand under the judgement of your over-arching love and righteousness. We thank you for those who were in former times our enemies, but are now our friends. Grant that the work of reconciliation may now bring lasting peace to the South Atlantic, and justice and security for all the peoples of the earth; for Jesus Christ's sake. Amen.

We said the Lord's Prayer, the Archbishop of Canterbury gave the blessing, we stood and sang the national anthem and the processions went slowly through the cathedral to the sunshine of Ludgate Hill. Some serious-eyed children left their seats to be close to the Queen and the Duke of Edinburgh as they processed down the cathedral and some in the processions were moved to tears by the sight of the children who had lost fathers, uncles and brothers.

Reactions – Critical and Affirming

The BBC one o'clock news reported that some MPs were critical. The next day there was strong criticism especially from some politicians and journalists. 'More suitable for Buenos Aires' (Julian Amery). 'The Archbishop was unspeakable and ought to resign' (one MP, unnamed). Dr Runcie revealed 'a failure of leadership' and Dr Greet's prayers were 'silly' (Dean of a Cambridge College). It felt as if a cold war had been declared on the churches.

Other journalists were quick to reply. The Editor in Chief of the Press Association wrote that everyone he had spoken to considered the service to be thoroughly appropriate and the Archbishop's sermon deeply moving. Sir Denis Hamilton, CO of an infantry battalion in the Normandy battles and Editor in Chief of *The Times*, thought the Archbishop deserved a bar to his MC. The service moved him 'more than anything I can remember. So appropriate at *every* point.' A former Governor of the Falklands and Brigadier Peter Young wrote in the same strain. A member of the House of Lords put it like this: 'I do not remember ever having felt so proud of the Church of England as I did this morning.' Two previous Prime Ministers, Alec Douglas-Home and James Callaghan, said it was a 'splendid service thanks to the hard work and sensitivity of St Paul's together with Hume and Greet . . . It inspired the huge congregation. Those who came with loss and sorrow will feel sustained and comforted all their lives.'

Those present in St Paul's as mourners or former combatants were positive. The widow of a Flight Commander killed on HMS *Ardent* with 22 other men wrote:

It was hard to believe, with such a congregation in one of the most beautiful cathedrals, that a service could promote such sincerity – there was no doubt that the people who were near to me and all the people who attended the service were so deeply moved by the very true words which were spoken.

A paratrooper at the service reflecting twelve years later wrote: 'I realised that the Archbishop had been right in 1982 but I did not think so at the time.'

The armed forces had begun the process of reconciliation. Lt David Tinker, who was killed when his ship HMS *Glamorgan* was the victim of an Exocet attack, two days before the surrender of the Argentinian forces, had expressed opposition to the war to his ship-mates – a tribute to their forbearance.

Work pressure and economic sanctions are quite enough for solving the dispute over a rock with a village population. It's just a question of which flag flies . . . Still, I suppose this is all an experience one should go through if only to drive home for each generation how stupid war is . . . Here certainly the material things are unimportant and human 'things', values and ways of life are thought about by everybody.

A naval captain reports:

I have been overwhelmed by the bravery of many men, especially those who suffered the most serious injuries. Injured Paras and Marines have been seen quietly helping Argentinian patients.

Captain Barker, of the survey ship HMS *Endurance*, noted how inconsistent it was of the British Government to combine a decision that the Falkland Islanders' wishes must be paramount and at the same time withdraw the British naval presence and not deploy a submarine – as had been done in the seventies. He asked Lt Commander Bicam of the submarine *Santa Fe*, which the navy had just captured, why the Argentinian submarine did not shoot a torpedo when it had a chance to sink *Endurance*. The Argentinian commander replied: 'I don't know really, but it may have had something to do with the excellent cocktail party you gave us at Mar del Plata.' Both navies obeyed their civilian governments but sought to avoid loss of life in the icy Antarctic around the islands of South Georgia, where there is the additional hazard of the mountains rising like the Alps but straight from the ocean. This did not mean that the crew of *Endurance* did not condemn the 'really nasty' Commander Aztiz, the Argentinian in charge of South Georgia, who had been responsible for the deaths of hundreds of left-wing activists under the tyrannous regime. One of *Endurance* ship's company, who had once been a chorister at St Paul's, kept in touch with the cathedral and came to be married there when peace returned.

Vincent Bramley, a paratrooper who was at the service, has recently spent time in the homes and the barracks of the Argentinian units he fought. His own account, dedicated to his children, includes a list of British and Argentinian losses on Mount Longdon and Wireless Ridge. 'I could see both sides. I saw the need to put aside questions of race, colour, religion and politics.' That was why, as already noticed, he came to believe that the Archbishop had been right in 1982. He ends by quoting an Argentinian mother, Hazel Altiere: 'I cried inside. I cried outside. I cried until I could cry no more.'

An agnostic outside all the churches wrote about the service:

> I am so moved by the moral triumph of the Falklands Service that I feel impelled to write. The whole tone of the administration's view of the Falklands Campaign seems to have presented our nation in a false jingoistic light, and whereas one can feel nothing but pride and gratitude to our forces for accomplishing their dangerous mission with outstanding courage, and so swiftly – it needed a moral force, such as the Church, to 'put the record straight'. It is deeply heart-warming to feel the strength of the Church, expressing a view shared by so many and so wonderfully expressed by the Pope. I admire Dr Runcie's courage in quoting those inspiring words in his sermon, and hope you will allow me (although agnostic) to thank you with all sincerity.

The service was a message from the churches to modern Britain, urging the gentler direction our country should take. The Church of England is not an instrument of state, even though it is still established. It is not the church's role to bless the status quo – whether Conservative or Labour. The churches, to quote the American theologian Richard Niebuhr, do not believe in 'a God without wrath, who brought men without sin, into a kingdom without judgment through the ministrations of a church without the cross'.

The Christian conviction that war is not God's method of settling international disputes had to be expressed. The courage of the Task

Force, thanksgiving that the Islanders had been rescued, and that a brutal dictator had been forced to resign was gratefully acknowledged, but the spiritual vision of swords being beaten into ploughshares and Wilfred Owen's poetic insights, from the much bloodier fields of France, of 'war and the pity of war' had to be the heart of the message – as they had not been in earlier imperial services at St Paul's.

Grief for mourners in Britain and Argentina took precedence over a victory parade. The message of the British churches got through to Buenos Aires. Bunches of flowers with Spanish inscriptions and the names of young men arrived in St Paul's. Copies of the service were requested by churches in South America. British business visitors to Argentina were personally befriended when they joined Roman Catholic worship. One Protestant visiting Sunday worship in Buenos Aires was asked to lead an offertory procession at the Mass. Correspondence came to St Paul's about renewed contacts; it felt as if the cathedral had become a tiny foreign office for a ministry of reconciliation.

Years later the body of an Argentinian pilot was found with his plane in a remote area of the Islands. His father flew from Buenos Aires to London to fly to the Falklands to visit the grave (a more direct route was impossible). The father purchased two wreaths in London and brought them both to St Paul's for me to bless. One he left at the South Atlantic memorial in the crypt of St Paul's; the other he took with him on his long journey of grief to lay on his son's grave in the Islands. Other Argentinians have continued to write and remember St Paul's as a 'mercy seat' for reconciliation. The South Atlantic memorial lists British dead but is in memory of all those who fell in the conflict. It has since been visited by the Prime Ministers of Argentina and Britain who together prayed in silence.

What Did It Mean?

Fortunately for the churches – Anglican, Roman, Free Church – and for the pacifist group in each, there was the chance for representatives to pray together, think together, to listen to each other and decide together. Denominational differences dissolved. Each recognized and valued the convictions and character of the others. We came to trust, and to like each other, and the common task of delivering a difficult message without alienating those who disagreed built up a warm relationship. Under the eyes of world television the churches in Britain were prepared to face unpopularity with some powerful and self designated patriotic forces for the sake of what they believed to be right.

There was less insistence on precedence among the churches. St Paul's chapter no longer expected to write or speak all the prayers. A woman was among the readers: so often national services have been all male. A Cardinal Archbishop was prepared to wait for co-operation for the wording of prayers from a Moderator temporarily out of touch in the Outer Isles. In July 1982 the church leaders let go their dignity and worked together to evolve a new relationship of ecumenical service.

Lay people from the different churches were prepared to take a responsible role. Decisions were not simply clerical. After the initial meeting in the Deanery on 30 June the Ministry of Defence was represented by Sir Arthur Hockaday who understood, as Sir Robin Day in a critical interview with me famously did not, why such hymns as 'Fight the Good Fight' and 'Onward Christian Soldiers' were inappropriate. When Sir Francis Pym, who succeeded Lord Carrington as Foreign Secretary, published his personal testament, he wrote:

> I do not see how the Church can stand aside from politics, I do not see how individual churchmen can ignore such profound moral issues as nuclear weapons. Clergymen do not exist to make life comfortable for us.
> (*Politics of Consent*, Hamish Hamilton, 1984, p. 29)

Immediately after the service a former Prime Minister, Sir Alec Douglas-Home, came to the Deanery to offer his support to the Task Force chaplains who had gathered there after they had said goodbye to the mourners. The church, Home and Pym insisted, is a defence against totalitarian tendencies in the modern state. These laymen wanted a dynamic, even aggressive church, able to stand in practice for God's deep love for the whole of humanity.

The storm which blew up over the Falklands Service left the British churches prepared to face criticism, and confident that the judgement of God must be sought in human affairs. They prayed for the Spirit's power to enable them to share the mind and the cross of Christ. It felt as if Christ was changing his church and uniting it to take risks. They rejoiced at the fall of General Galtieri and recognized the Task Force's role in his overthrow. But the churches had also to proclaim the way of reconciliation and world understanding.

An Argentinian poet ought to have the last word.

> They would have been friends but they met only once
> face to face on some too famous islands.
> And each one was Cain, and each one was Abel.
> They buried them together. Snow and corruption know them.
> The deed to which I refer took place in a time that we
> cannot understand.

(Jorge Luis Borges, Argentina's most famous man of letters, quoted in *British Argentinian Relations*, Chatham House, 1991)

We need to be able now to say together:

> Padre nuestro que estás en los cielos,
> Sanctificado sea tu nombre
> Que venga tu reino.
> Que se haga tu voluntad en la tierra, así
> Como se hace en el cielo.
> Danos hoy el pan que necesitamos.
> Perdónanos el mal que hemos hecho, así como
> Nosotros hemo perdonado a los que nos
> Han hecho mal.
> No nos pongas a prueba, sino líbranos de maligno.
> Porque tuyo es el reino, y el poder, y la gloria,
> Por siempre. Amén.

References

Barker, Nick, *Beyond Endurance*. Barnsley, Leo Cooper, 1997.
Bramley, Vincent, *Two Sides of Hell*. London, 22 Books, 1994.

Runcie, Robert, *Windows onto God*. London, SPCK, 1983. (Includes the full text of his Falklands sermon.)

Tinker, David, *A Message from the Falklands*. London, Penguin, 1983. (Especially pp. 122–211.)

World Council of Churches, *Conflict in the South Atlantic*. Geneva, WCC, 1983.

7 NEW LITURGIES:
Minting the Mystery

In my own lifetime it has felt as if the Christian conscience was bringing together the prayers of the different traditions within the churches. In the increasingly secularized West, those who believed themselves called to pray and to try to share the mind of Christ often found themselves in agreement in their criticism of contemporary society. Relief agencies, Catholic and Protestant, found themselves praying in almost the same words about issues of justice and peace, health and poverty. Theological teaching became a shared discipline both in universities and in theological colleges. At Lincoln where I worked in the 1960s, Methodist scholars were on the staff full time and Roman Catholic scholars for a term each year. We celebrated the Orthodox Liturgy annually – with much practice to be at home with the complex music. This unity in thinking and worship, both together and in private, greatly enriched our understanding of prayer. But we still felt that we had much to learn. Married priests bringing up families, sometimes in difficult environments, wondered later whether we had struggled enough to change the neo-monastic spirituality of theological colleges into a way of prayer more rooted, earthed, shared. Mark Tully, once an ordinand at Lincoln, now a writer in Delhi, has done much through his broadcasts 'Something Understood' to deepen and reinterpret spirituality.

While on holiday with my family camping in the Dordogne in the seventies, I was given another experience of the prayer of the future church. The camping site with its dozens of tents was largely blown away by a hurricane, and the nearby village of Marcillac-la-Croisille saved the situation by opening up their hall for the night. Afterwards we naturally wanted to repay their kindness. The Mayor, who was a doctor, welcomed our presence at his blood transfusion centre and the curé asked for my help at the next Sunday Mass. To my question 'What would the Bishop of Tulle say?' he replied, 'If he knew he would be glad.' So I concelebrated in a fullish church whose service in French was remarkably similar to the Parish Communions to which I was accustomed in England. After the service the curé left me to clear up as he had to motorbike urgently to Clermont-Ferrand where a village fireman was in hospital. I noted the curé had a photograph of Pope Paul VI and Archbishop Michael Ramsey together in a scene of reconciliation.

But some in all churches do not find change in worship easy or natural. Small symbols, even candles, become intensely controversial. An absurd scene took place long ago, in April 1897, at Gorleston near Yarmouth. My grandfather preserved the newspaper report, which reads as follows:

Extraordinary Scene in a Church
All in the Name of Religion.

The Bishop of Norwich attended for the annual confirmation service. When his Lordship emerged from the vestry with the clergy and choir, and entered the chancel, he observed lighted candles on the altar, and at once asked the Vicar, the Revd Forbes Phillips, to remove them. The Vicar curtly declined, and asserted his supreme authority in his own church.

The Bishop – I shall not proceed with the service unless the lights be removed.

Vicar – You may please yourself, but the lights shall remain.

His Lordship then directed the churchwardens to extinguish the candles. These officials, however, ranged themselves at the side of the Vicar, and one of them declared, 'We are not the servants of the Bishop, and have no authority beyond the altar rails.'

Bishop – I have a grave objection to lighted candles on the altar in the daytime, and probably the congregation share my views.

Vicar – I invite any such to declare themselves.

Bishop – I shall not conduct the service.

Vicar – (taking out his watch) I shall give you one minute to make up your mind, and if you then still refuse I shall conduct the service myself, ascend the pulpit, and declare the candidates members of the Church of England, throwing upon you the responsibility of rejecting them afterwards.

Before a minute had elapsed the bishop, who seemed intensely annoyed, elected, as he said, for the sake of peace, and to spare the feelings of the congregation, to proceed with the service; but the influences of the scene were painfully evident throughout the service. At the close instead of joining in the recessional procession, his Lordship sat in solitary state in the chancel.
(See J. Breay, *Fellside Parson*, p. 238)

Since then the Church has been on a steep learning curve about living with differences; bishops adapt to variety in worship as they travel round their dioceses. In many parishes worship groups exist, creating special services and exploring for themselves their understanding of liturgy and life.

Prayers no longer begin almost automatically with 'Almighty God'. For some this might conjure up an 'old man in the skies' with a literally true Bible in one threatening hand and an invariable Book of Common Prayer in the other. Today God is sought everywhere, especially in the depths of human personality and in the mysteries of life as we experience the twenty-first century. Some say this view is 'reductionist' – not adequate to the wonder and grandeur of God. But it brings near the hidden, utterly other, even in a world threatened by war, disease and pollution. We go on praying, together and also in those moments when we are alone and turn to the mysterious other within and behind our lives – the 'Beyond' within us.

Our worship now is often enriched by movement, drama or poetry. Our year 2000 *Common Worship* speaks in its preface of this generation and its need for imaginative engagement in worship. Long ago, in 1928, some of the 1662 prayers were amended or omitted as theology developed. The 1662 Prayer Book, in the Third Collect for Good Friday, enjoined us to pray that God would 'have mercy on all Jews, Turks, Infidels and Hereticks' and would take from them 'all ignorance, hardness of heart, and contempt of thy word'. In the century of world wars, the Holocaust and combatants with gas, chemical and nuclear arms, Christians became uneasy at this crusading spirit towards Jews and Muslims and the hostility towards those who disagreed with orthodoxy. Jesus himself was a Jew and many had thought him a Jewish heretic. As Christian theology grappled with modern disasters, people asked 'Where was God at Auschwitz?' 'Among the Jews, gypsies and homosexuals in the gas chambers' was the answer most believers gave.

Prayer at the beginning and end of life has always felt natural. We want to celebrate birth and name a baby, and to give thanks for a life which has ended. Even in the formality of a court of law when a court makes an adoption order there may be an informal expression of joy. The judge today may feel sufficiently relaxed to place his or her wig on the child's head and invite photographs. Some find this surprising, but welcome and happiness have to be at the heart of the adoption process. So also when a child is baptized welcome must be at the heart of the sacrament. All the family and friends, including those who might be called wistful agnostics – of which there may be many at such a service – need to feel that their convictions are respected, their experience recognized, even as they are invited to hear or say the Lord's Prayer and to come within the church building.

I am going to quote two family services, as I was involved in their creation. There are of course many special services being put together today for baptisms, weddings, funerals and local church occasions. Families, parish groups and the staff of cathedrals use poetry and often material from the Iona and Taizé Communities as well as the work of Janet Morley and Jim Cotter. Jean Mayland, one of the creators of the *Alternative Service Book 1980* and now an officer of Churches Together in Britain and Ireland (CTBI) has pointed out that it is unfortunate that this contemporary spirituality has been largely ignored by the compilers of *Common Worship*.

> We need to retrieve evocative images from the spirituality of the past to supplement biblical images and above all to discover new ways of imaging and describing God, which nurture the understanding of women and men in our world today. We need writing which is uncluttered and direct, but also poetic and stirring to the emotions ... That is why I say to my church with love ... find

new, inclusive, poetic language and symbolism from our own age to describe and worship God and meet the needs of the millions in this nation. Above all, be prepared to do this along with your fellow Christians in the other churches.

(*Modern Churchpeople's Newsletter*, March/April 2001)

It is not wilful idiosyncrasy, or any kind of iconoclasm about traditional words or beliefs, which leads to fresh symbols and ceremonies. It is a wish to be honest, to express some aspects of our collective understanding of faith and life. Today we may or may not choose an ancient building. Some choose a special natural setting, the banks of a river or a clearing in a wood, which can unite various convictions, humanist, agnostic and Christian. At high points in the year – Christmas, Easter, or harvest-time – people may especially wish to look at their lives in a new light.

Wiveton, a Norfolk village church once threatened with being closed as redundant, now complements its weekly worship with creative special services. People pack in as a flautist from the neighbouring village of Cley leads the congregation at Christmas to a baby, perhaps only a fortnight old, lying on straw beside the mother. At Easter the experienced miracle of resurrection life is shared in music and poetry as the gospel story is acted out and we give thanks for Jesus Christ.

The following services for baptism and for thanksgiving after a marriage were created after months of discussion and correspondence within my own family. In each case it was hoped we could bring something personal to the services and still be loyal to the traditions to which we owe so much. We did not see this as a rival to the official baptism liturgy or as normative for other families – it was an offering which worked for us and cost much thought and discussion.

The first service was created by fusing the core elements of baptism in the name of God and the signing with the sign of the cross of Jesus Christ, with fresh poetry and symbolism. We gathered in a circle in the ruins outside the church, with the North Sea just over the horizon, and then moved inside. The parents, grandparents and vicar had thought out the form of the service together and one of the friends, the poet Nick Drake, read his own welcoming poem for

William. It seemed good that in and around an eleventh-century church there was so much music, poetry and movement and that the friends took such an active share in affirming and welcoming the baby.

Service of Baptism at Binham Priory, 8 July, 1998

THE WELCOME

When members of the family and friends are gathered in the ruins of Binham Priory, the baby's grandfather, a priest, introduces the service:

The birth of a child is a joyous and solemn occasion in the life of a family. It is also an occasion of rejoicing among friends. I bid you, therefore, to join Justin and Catherine in giving thanks for the gift of William Munro to be their son.

They have chosen this romantic, amazing and atmospheric place – a church without a roof, open to the sky, open to past, present and future. It was a place of active life in the past; there were bakeries and a refectory, a dormitory, a hospital and a place of hospitality. Today it is open to rain and sun, thunderstorms and wind. It is a peaceful place where we meet to welcome a young life which has the future before it.

The baby's mother　　welcomes those present
　　　　　　　　　　　and speaks about the baby's names

THE READINGS

The mother　　　　　　From *The Prophet*, by Kahlil Gibran

Your children are not your children.
They are the sons and daughters of Life's longing for itself
They come through you but not from you
And, though they are with you, yet they belong not to you.

You may give them your love, but not your thoughts

For they have their own thoughts.
You may house their bodies but not their spirits
For their spirits dwell in the house of tomorrow.
You may strive to be like them but seek not to make them
    like you.
For life goes not backward nor tarries with yesterday.
You are the bows from which your children as living arrows
    are sent forth.

The father   From *The Firstborn* by Laurie Lee, adapted
                    for a son.

What have I got exactly? And what am I going to do with him?
And what for that matter will he do with me? I have got a son,
whose life is already separate from mine, whose will already follows
its own directions, and who has quickly corrected my woolly pre-
conceptions of him by being something remorselessly different.
He is the child of himself and will be what he is. I am merely the
keeper of his temporary helplessness. Even so, with luck, he can
alter me; indeed, is doing so now. At this stage in my life he will
give me more than he gets, and may even later become *my* keeper.
But if I could teach him anything at all – I'd like it to be acceptance
and a holy relish for life.

Given this world to be in, where he can grow reasonably
wild . . . I hope he'll be free from fear to enquire and get answers,
free to imagine and tell tall tales, free to be curious and to show
enthusiasm, and free at times to be invaded by silences.

A special friend   Adapted from Dorothy Law Nolte

Children Learn What They Live

If a child lives with tolerance, he learns to be patient;
If a child lives with encouragement, he learns confidence;
If a child lives with praise, he learns to appreciate;
If a child lives with fairness, he learns judgment;
If a child lives with acceptance and friendship, he learns to
    give love to the world.

PRAYER, said by all

May the power of air bring you a clear mind to see your way
May the power of fire bring you strength and passion to go
   along your way
May the power of water bring you life and sustenance, and the
   courage to feel your way
May the power of earth bring you grounding in a strong body,
   to be centred in your way.

All now move inside the Priory Church (the nave of the monastery) and sit down near the front.

MUSIC

SILENCE

THE POEM (printed at end of chapter)

THE CEREMONY OF LIGHT AND CANDLES

The priest speaks briefly about the symbolism of baptism. When William was born he was welcomed, washed and clothed. In baptism all these three elements are present. Thinking of the importance of family and friends the priest remembered with pleasure that he was taught by the baby's great-grandfather.

Candles are distributed then lit, one from another, in a semi-circle. The water is prepared.

The priest Bless these waters of your new creation. May we be renewed, walk in the light of faith and serve in newness of life.

The mother presents the baby to the priest who asks the parents to name their child. The parents reply.

The priest William Munro, I baptize you, in the name of the Eternal Spirit Life-Giver, Redeemer, Inspirer.
   I sign you with the sign of the Cross.

Loving God, look with favour on this child; grant that, being nourished with all goodness, he may grow in discipline and grace until he comes to the fullness of his own faith. Amen.

The Lord's Prayer, followed by a Blessing said by all:

> Bless your eyes that you may have
> clarity of vision,
> Bless your mouth that you may speak
> the truth,
> Bless your ears that you may hear
> all that is spoken to you,
> Bless your heart that you may be
> filled with love,
> Bless your feet that you may find and walk
> your own true path.
> Amen.

During the service there was a profound sense of commitment to the spiritual growth and well-being of the baby. The power of the sacrament of baptism, in our need for life, forgiveness and resurrection, was strongly felt. After the ceremony the baby's names were entered in the baptism register by the Vicar, John Penny, who also presented him with a gift from the churchwardens.

Not only services of baptism or naming, but also marriage services need special thought. The churches have discussed for generations what form of prayer they will offer for a second marriage or for the increasing number of couples who are married at a civil ceremony but wish for prayers afterwards. It has sometimes felt as if more time was spent in church circles making clear that marriage was intended to be for life than in securing a blessing on the new relationship that is beginning and needs the gift of God's grace. Sometimes the couple wish the time of prayer to be private; sometimes they want it to be an occasion when their families can be together and pray together. Always they hope for a ceremony which expresses the integrity of their new relationship with an imaginative drawing on the treasures of their religious traditions.

Here is a service used in May 1998 for my son Stephen and

daughter-in-law Giovanna, who had been married in a civil ceremony in Italy. They came from the Roman Catholic and Church of
England traditions and had many Jewish friends. They chose the
medieval church of Cley-next-the-Sea already well known to them
from holidays. They decided that the ceremony should be quiet; no
others were invited but the rector gave permission for this blessing
to take place. It was a still morning with blossom, birdsong and a
strong sense of gratitude. The light streamed through the clear glass
of the east window of the church.

Service of Blessing at St Margaret's Church, Cley, *3 May, 1998*

We begin standing round the font, the place of life-giving water.

The priest, who is father of the bridegroom: a prayer remembering
their baptisms, one at Barnard Castle baptised by Bishop John
Ramsbotham and the other in Siena. We give thanks for their
journey so far, their faithful love, and their search for truth and for
the way.

We pray for our families in all the changes and chances of their
lives. Enable us to stay in touch with one another, learning from
and supporting one another, across the generations from the age-
ing to the new-born. Grant us to grow in courage, humour, compassion, generosity and insight, so that together we may come to
your eternal Kingdom of light and joy.

The bridegroom's mother: We are part of a great human pilgrimage; we remember those with whom we are most intimately
bound up, our families, our friends, our mentors and guides, all
those who have loved and cared about us, living and departed.

(Names may be said aloud)

God of intimacy
you surround us with friends and family
to cherish and to challenge:

May we so give and receive caring
in the details of our lives
that we also remain faithful
to your greater demands,
through Jesus Christ, Amen.

We go up the aisle and stand near the pulpit and lectern, the places for reading, teaching and reflection.

The groom, Stephen, reads a passage from Tolstoy's *War and Peace* in which Count Bezukhov and Prince Andrei discuss the purpose of life.

The bride, Giovanna, reads from Thomas à Kempis' *The Imitation of Christ* Book III, Chapter V, Section 3.

Love is a great thing, yes, a great and thorough Good; by itself it makes everything that is heavy, light; and it bears evenly all that is uneven.
For it carries a burden which is no burden, and makes every thing that is bitter, sweet and tasteful.
The noble love of Jesus impels a man to do great things, and stirs him up to be always longing for what is more perfect.
Love desires to be aloft, and will not be kept back by any thing low and mean.
Love desires to be free, and estranged from all worldly affections, that so its inward sight may not be hindered; that it may not be entangled by any temporal prosperity, or by any adversity subdued.
Nothing is sweeter than Love, nothing more courageous, nothing higher, nothing wider, nothing more pleasant, nothing fuller nor better in Heaven and earth; because Love is born of God, and cannot rest but in God, above all created things.

We go through the choir to the altar steps. The bride and groom stand at the steps.

The priest This is the place of blessing. First we will bless the wedding ring, a circle with no beginning and no end, an outward and visible sign of an inward and spiritual bond which unites your hearts in love. It represents your love for each other, a love which began in trust, has grown through companionship and deepened with understanding.

Bless this ring, O merciful Lord, that he who gives it and she who wears it may both be faithful and may abide in your love till their lives' end.

The couple kneel at the altar

The priest Remembering our Jewish friends, we use a prayer from the Jewish marriage service:

Lord, who taught men and women to help and serve each other in marriage, and lead each other into happiness, bless this covenant of affection, these promises of truth. Protect and care for Stephen and Giovanna as they go through life together. May they be loving companions, secure in their devotion with the passing years. In their respect and honour for each other may they find their peace and, in their affection and tenderness, their happiness. May your presence be in their home and in their hearts. Amen.

The Lord's Prayer (in English or Italian)

The priest Go in peace
and may God the Mother keep you safe
God in Christ take you by the hand
And God the Spirit cover you with her warm, bright
wings.

Liturgies of Hope and Change

Prayer often arises at times of rapid change or of frustration. Margaret Webster, in *A New Strength, A New Song*, writes of the life-giving prayer that developed within the Movement for the Ordination of Women as the years rolled on.

For many women and men within MOW, the on-going prayer enfolding its life was something of a revelation. The first 'Wilderness Liturgies', often held out of doors, were born out of alienation and pain but were strangely strengthening, with their sharing of milk and honey cake and strong sense of the hope and faith of an exiled community.

These, together with ongoing groups and gatherings,

were like the first planks in a raft of prayer which was to uphold the life of the Movement for years. As well as the great national occasions in Westminster Abbey, Canterbury and Coventry cathedrals, each diocese had a particular day of the month for remembering their women deacons and all our hopes.

In Norwich diocese, for instance, there was prayer and lighting of candles in fifteen villages or towns on the ninth day of each month. And new forms of worship were explored, new liturgies thought about, with freshness and creativity.

At other times, a Novena of Prayer was used. In 1989 the first day, on Faithful Discipleship, included this prayer:

Holy Mother and Father of us all, Help us to open to your love as the birds welcome the new day; Give us the courage to abandon ourselves to your adoring love, knowing that you, who have been faithful from the beginning of time are bringing us to see you face to face. Give us openness, Lord, to pray For all that has been, Thanks, For all that shall be, Yes.

It closed with a prayer by Janet Morley from her collection of collects *All Desires Known*:

O God, for whom we long as a woman in labour longs for her delivery; give us the courage to wait, strength to push and discernment to know the right time, that we may bring into the world your joyful peace, through Jesus Christ. Amen.

The whole Novena is a model of earthed writing, devised by a trio of women in Southampton, Ann Lewin, Eileen Wetherall and Bridget Woollard.

Another Novena was written for the nine days before the final General Synod vote in 1992. The prayer on the fifth day also uses both old and new imagery:

> God our Mother and Father, Living Water, River of Mercy, Source of Life, in whom we live and move and have our being, who quenches our thirst, and refreshes our weariness, bathes and washes and cleanses our wounds; be for us always a fountain of life and for all the world a river of hope springing up in the midst of the deserts of despair. Honour and blessing, glory and praise to You for ever. Amen.

Over the last 25 years, therefore, new thinking on the language of prayer has been emerging. Much of this has been ignored by the churches, but it has been influential among women and men praying at home or in informal groups. Brian Wren, a United Reformed Church minister, published in 1989 *What Language Shall I Borrow? God-Talk in Worship; a Male Response to Feminist Theology.* He points to the maleness of so much in the western naming of God. Much traditional praying addressed a patriarchal God. Wren used the word KING-FATHER-ALL-POWERFUL (Kingafap) as a blanket description of this approach. (Even the new Anglican *Common Worship* strikes the user as astonishingly male in most of the adjectives and imagery of God.) Wren also pointed out that often courage is described in exclusively male terms; he quotes as typical a writer in *The Economist* on the 1986 USA bombing raid on Libya who wrote, 'Maggie Thatcher is the only head of government in Western Europe who has balls'. In this way courage is expressed solely in terms of masculinity, as if there were not women all over the world showing immense courage, strong in themselves and as women.

Many reshape their language of prayer about God as the years go by. William Blake's old description of everyone praying in distress and thankfulness 'To Mercy, Pity, Peace and Love' seems to describe our longing for compassion. God is within the boys and girls, Arabs and Jews, as they are killed in Palestine. The horrors of contemporary history seem to draw us away from prayer to an almighty king or powerful authoritarian father, to pray within a Spirit-filled world, confident that God is in fact beyond words. The old tradition of the basic unknowability of God (the way of talking of apophatic theology in Eastern Christian thought) may help churches to avoid being so cocksure about divine names and the divine will.

Where pressures block the liberation of humanity, in my own experience the subject of prayer must face the harsh reality in which so many people live. English society in the eighties was torn by riots in Brixton, Bristol, Liverpool and elsewhere. The race relations unit of the British Council of Churches organized a service in St Paul's for the Black-led British Churches with their own preacher and intercessors. About 20 of their own bishops, magnificently robed, and other lead- ers, brought 1,500 of their flocks, and London's white Christians came too in their hundreds. Prayer, dance, preaching and hymns were all shared. I was moved by the sense of divine blessing on a new and at times difficult multi-ethnic society born amidst such apathy and some hostility.

I find my prayers arise from my struggles. Perhaps prayer books like *Common Worship* feel like wheelbarrows, full of resources, valu- able but not always relevant. I warm to the prayer books which face more directly the pressures which can be so depressing. *All Desires Known* (1988), which faces the anti-feminine problems of the churches; *Bread of Tomorrow: Praying with the World's Poor* (1992) sponsored by Christian Aid; *Human Rites: Worship Resources from an Age of Change* (1995) and the beautifully illustrated *Dear Life* (1998), praying through the year with Christian Aid. The powerful atmospheric photographs inspire a conversion of the heart and imagination. And in Jim Cotter's Cairns Publications and his medi- tations *Dazzling Darkness* and *Prayers at Night* (a new form of Compline) many find encouragement in their pilgrimage. Even for those of us who are truly nourished by the daily on-going worship of the church, the regular centuries-old pattern of the priest saying the daily office, or the people of God gathering week by week, newly minted language and imagery may be a necessary part of their search for reality in prayer. That is my experience.

Especially powerful are prayers where the words are accompanied by symbolic action. The Eucharist is for us the supreme example. The drama of inter-faith services is also symbolic. In July 1999 Christianity and Islam, in spite of a long history of conflict, joined in an English/Arabic Service in St Paul's to remember King Hussein of Jordan. In the words of the Prince of Wales, who gave a profoundly humane address, King Hussein was

> a faithful follower of Islam, a man among men and a King among Kings . . . who had the kind of enlightened spirit which was in harmony with those who in earlier periods of history, were able instructively to respect the followers of other faiths even if they did not accept them theologically.

The Prince contrasted our own age where we witness appalling acts of brutality – mass murder, genocide and ethnic cleansing. The Dean led 'the different traditions of faith' in prayer. When King Abdullah read from the Qur'an he included the passage 'We do not differentiate between any of His messengers'. Here was prayer and reflection in action with members of different faiths gathered round God's altar under the dome.

The Millennium Service for Londoners at St Paul's on 8 January 2000 was also a prayer of unity in action said by many different churches and many world faith communities. Led by Perpetual Beauty and students of the Italia Conti Academy, 'The River of Time', they filled the cathedral with song, movement and music before the Millennium Resolution was sung: 'Let there be respect for the earth, peace for its people, love in our lives, delight in the good, forgiveness for past wrongs and from now on a new start'. The combination of prayer, pageant, music and movement seemed to express hope in a fresh start for London. The colours, youth, sheer exuberance of their dancing in the amazing spaces of St Paul's transformed the cathedral. There was not a single prayer beginning 'Almighty God' and none of the stuffiness which sometimes creeps into state services. It felt as if the church was at last accepting the many world faith communities in all their varieties and not asking for submission to the language of 'miserable sinners'. The Millennium prayers had a 'tingle factor' which can reopen the church to the story of our times and the language of our day.

Prayer lives in a particular way when it is understood in the context of the struggle for justice, compassion, liberation and love. We try to share in God's attention to humanity, in all its tragedies and joys. I felt this when worshipping in a camp set up by the church in El Salvador to rescue campesinos – the peasants and their children – from the civil war. They had been supported by their bishop who had been on the side of liberation. In their prayers they called him St Oscar Romero. On the day I spent in that camp, I knelt with a Jesuit priest, a Catholic sister, a Baptist and a Methodist minister and an Anglican laywoman, and we all received communion together under the trees. The prayers at that wooden table seemed to link one back to the first communion in Jerusalem and forward to God's reign on earth. It seemed natural that the priest who celebrated should come a few years later to join us in prayer at St Paul's and to share in our midday Eucharist.

When it was time in December 1987 to say goodbye to St Paul's and to many duties, friends, half our books and the delights of living in London, and return to the joys of Norwich and Norfolk, we were grateful for many gifts and among them this contemporary prayer from Janet Morley. It spoke to my needs and I often send it to others on their retirement, and use it for myself.

Blessing for those laying down office

> May the God who rested on the seventh day
> to delight in all her creation,
> hold you in her arms
> as you have held this work,
> celebrate with us
> the life that takes life from you,
> and give you grace to let go
> into a new freedom. Amen.

Minting the Mystery is never simply a question of finding the right words. A member of the Wantage Community once said that God had perhaps an impish way of hiding within ourselves, and others, and everything. We do not have to formulate correct descriptions in words as if we were involved in a court conversation which must begin with the proper name. We live and move and have our being with the Mystery within and around – a Mystery, to use the old formulas, more Transcendent and more Immanent than we can imagine, let alone define in words. So that often we seek the Mystery in silence, we rest in contemplation.

Poem for a Baby

Take these gifts,
put on your life;
The spinning top of your heart
The mirror-ball of light
The music box of days

While the world still sleeps
come into the quiet
Of Saturday morning at 3 am;
Hush, don't cry,
Listen to the bird song
Of here and now

Wake from your long dream
To more of everything,
To the first morning light
In the window,
To the changing sky,
The grey sea and the shining sea,
The laughing seals,
The white manes of the sea horses,
And the lost carnelian
Found in the open hand of the waves
As you are found
For us at last
Here and now
Dressed in a gown

Older than the century
and lighter than this morning's light

Now is your time; have no fear;
Remember the song you knew before;
take these gifts, put on your life
And meet your mother
Waiting and hoping;
Hold her hand,
Put on love
The secret crown
And answer to your name

William

© Nick Drake

References

Breay, John, *A Fellside Parson: Joseph Brunskill and his Diaries, 1826–1903*. Norwich, Canterbury Press, 1995.

Cotter, Jim, *Dazzling Darkness: Cairns for a Journey*. Sheffield, Cairns in association with Arthur James, 1999.

Ecclestone, Alan, *Gather the Fragments*. Sheffield, Cairns, 1993.

à Kempis, Thomas, *The Imitation of Christ*. Oxford, John Henry Parker, 1853.

McRae-McMahon, Dorothy, *Prayers for Life's Particular Moments*. London, SPCK, 2001.

Morley, Janet, *All Desires Known*. London, SPCK, 1992.

Morley, Janet, *Bread of Tomorrow*. London, SPCK, 1992.

Morley, Janet, *Dear Life*. London, Christian Aid, 1998.

Ward, Hannah, and Wild, Jennifer, *Human Rites*. London, Mowbray, 1995.

Webster, Margaret, *A New Strength, a New Song: the Journey to Women's Priesthood*. London, Mowbray, 1994.

Williams, Harry, *The True Wilderness*. London, Constable, 1965.

Wren, Brian, *What Language Shall I Borrow?* London, SCM Press, 1989.

Also many liturgies written by members of the Movement for the Ordination of Women.

8 DIETRICH BONHOEFFER: The Blood Test of Faith

Choose and do what is right, not what fancy takes,
not weighing the possibilities, but bravely grasping the real,
not in the flight of ideas, but only in action is there freedom.
Come away from your anxious hesitations into the storm
of events,
carried by God's command and your faith alone.
Then freedom will embrace your spirit with rejoicing.

(Dietrich Bonhoeffer, trans. E. Robertson, in *Voices in the Night*)

In the summer of 1998 a unique congregation gathered in Westminster Abbey – perhaps the most impressive congregation of believers ever assembled in London. They came from all continents and many countries: Russia, South Africa, Poland, New Guinea, Germany, Pakistan, the USA, Uganda and El Salvador. They were the relations, friends and supporters of martyrs in the twentieth century. They belonged to many different denominations, and because many martyrs are unpublicized, their invitations called for much research. The violent twentieth century had witnessed more martyrs in the church than any century since the time of Jesus Christ. Ten of the martyr figures were carved in stone and set in that very public London space – over the west door of Westminster Abbey.

It was an anxious and delicate task for the main researchers (Dr Andrew Chandler, Director of the George Bell Institute, Canon Anthony Harvey of Westminster Abbey and Sister Hilary of Wantage) to choose the martyrs, and for the sculptors to create their likenesses. But in that service on 9 July 1998, in the presence of the Queen (herself a relative of one of the martyrs, the Grand

Duchess Elizabeth of Russia) the authority of 'the noble army of martyrs' made itself felt. The German cellist Dietrich Bethge, godson of Dietrich Bonhoeffer, played a haunting Bach Sarabande. Margaret Dehqani-Tafti, whose son Bahram William was killed in Iran in 1980, read St Paul's words: 'We do not lose heart . . . what is seen is transient, what is unseen is eternal' (2 Corinthians 4.16–18, REB). Fellow Polish Franciscans had come to honour Maximilian Kolbe, who died at Auschwitz; Americans came to honour Martin Luther King; Africans came for Manche Masemola. An associated commemorative concert and overnight hospitality as well as the act of worship itself enabled this gathering of 'the holy common people of God' to acknowledge those whose faith met the ultimate test, and who gave their lives. They fulfilled the prophecy of Martin Luther King: 'We shall hew out of the mountains of despair a stone of hope.'

Religious truth has always been most clearly communicated through personalities. Creeds, forms of worship, moral codes and hierarchical authorities are secondary. For those within the Christian tradition, saints and martyrs – especially the communion of saints among our contemporaries – are primary evidence for religious reality in an increasingly complicated and scientific world. According to Bonhoeffer, we as Christians see 'our own death as the festival' in which we hand over our spirit to the Creator Spirit. We are wise to learn all we can from the saints and martyrs of our time.

Martin Luther King, Oscar Romero and Dietrich Bonhoeffer, all within the Christian tradition, have much in common. They valued the various churches in which they were trained but regarded them as secondary. For them all, the transcendent was supremely revealed in their neighbours, and the divine call which cost them their lives was justice to their neighbour and the building of a gentler, more compassionate society. All looked to the future to vindicate the struggles of their lives, in which they met so much cruelty and repression. All three prayed and worshipped but were also active in the search for justice. None has more to teach the churches today than the European martyr Dietrich Bonhoeffer.

The main facts of Dietrich Bonhoeffer's life can be quickly told. Born in Berlin in 1905, the son of a university professor who was an authority on psychiatry and neurology, he was brought up in a cultivated liberal family, proud of the fact that a great grandfather on one side and a grandfather on the other side had both been dismissed for their liberal opinions. One had corrected Kaiser Wilhelm II for referring to the workers as 'rabble'. Bonhoeffer's father was agnostic about religion but believed in encouraging his seven children to make up their own minds. Bonhoeffer's family life was intelligent, secure and warm, despite the disasters of World War I and the upheavals and inflation which followed it. An intriguing story is told of how one of the children dropped a toy on the floor during a train journey. Such were the family standards of hygiene that his mother instantly opened the window and threw the toy from the train, to the huge distress of the child.

Dietrich Bonhoeffer decided at the age of 14 to be a theologian, and had a brilliant academic career. Significantly, his university thesis at Berlin was on the theme of the communion of saints. He then worked as a pastor in Germany but later lived in Barcelona, London, New York and Rome, so that the worldwide church was grafted into his understanding of Christianity. It is this strand in his training, in addition to the inherited family liberalism, which made him suspicious of attempts by Hitler and his followers to suggest that Christianity was basically anti-Semitic. Bonhoeffer realized that to see Hitler as a kind of god meant, in practice, the total rejection of the Old Testament and the spirit of the Sermon on the Mount. He was one of the very first to rebut the attack on the Jews and to denounce it as essentially anti-Christian. In 1933, six years before World War II, he began the formation within the Lutheran Church of a confessional church to withstand the attempts of the State to control the Church. He joined the resistance to Hitler, rejected pacifism, and was one of the group (though by then already in prison) who attempted (but failed) to assassinate the Führer on 20 July 1944. He spent the last two years of his life in prison and was executed on 9 April 1945 at the age of 39, on the direct orders of Himmler, the head of the secret police, a few days before the American troops arrived to liberate the prison. His brother and both his brothers-in-law were executed at the same time.

Bonhoeffer's background in the German traditions of the Lutheran Church, so interwoven with the state, may make his struggle seem obscure and irrelevant to the twenty-first century. But he saw himself and his fellow Christians confronted with, in his own words, a 'terrible alternative of either willing the defeat of their own nation in order that Christian civilization may survive or willing the victory of their nation and thereby destroying our civilization'. This struggle between nationalistic advantage and Christian civilization, though fortunately for Britain in less extreme form, was at the root of the controversies about *Faith in the City* and the Falklands Islands service discussed earlier, and will remain at the heart of the claims of Christianity to contribute to humanity.

Bonhoeffer was a man of prayer, a pastor with unusual gifts of friendliness as well as a theologian of great ability. Though he was prepared to be involved in gritty church administration, he distrusted 'churchiness', the attitudes of what he called 'the religious person'. As he grew older he became less church-centred and began to wonder whether in Germany ministers should earn their own living and be free of all state control.

He prayed for a return to faith in God for the sake of the whole of human life, not in order to restore the power base of the institutional churches. Though his own experience had given him a rare grasp of the resources of western European Christendom, including Rome, he also developed an admiration for the reality of religion in the East. Had he survived he would certainly have visited Gandhi. He would have been as much at home in an ashram or a monastery as he was in a Protestant pulpit.

He became more concerned with justice as he grew older. At his trial he admitted he was an implacable enemy of National Socialism. He fought against the exclusion from the ordained ministry of Jews who had become Christians. He saw the persecution of the Jews as a hideous crime against which every Christian must fight. God had spoken through Jewish prophets, and chosen a Jew, Jesus Christ, as his Son. Many Christians both Protestant and Catholic admired his courage but questioned his discretion. Some, like Martin Niemöller the former World War I boat commander, went to prison but did not take Bonhoeffer's decision to join in the attempt to assassinate Hitler.

German Christendom on the whole failed to denounce the

genocide of the Jews and afterwards felt guilty. Visiting Germany in 1946, after the war, I remember walking through the streets of Cassel which was almost totally demolished during the American and British bombing. I remarked to my host, a pastor, as he described the fire storm which destroyed the centre of the city, that he must feel bitter against the British and Americans for this indiscriminate destruction. He quietly replied, 'No, I do not feel bitter. I see it as a divine judgement. I stood in these very streets in 1937, when the Jews of Cassel were paraded in their thousands and we all turned out to watch as they were led away, pelted and insulted by their neighbours and fellow citizens. I remarked to my wife as we stood at the back of the crowd, "God will judge us for this."'

The ambiguities of European history, the Communists pressing against Eastern Germany and the memory of the harsh Versailles settlement, were skilfully exploited by the National Socialist machine to prevent all but the very clear-sighted and the very brave from making protests. Bonhoeffer's stand was based on absolute obedience to the biblical revelation of God's love for humanity. He accepted a costly discipleship and was suspicious of 'cheap grace', of those cosy flatteries which can infect pious language. 'As God chose the Jews, it is for us to see in them the Divine Spirit at work.' Bonhoeffer came to speak without ambiguity: 'Only one who cries for the Jews may sing Gregorian chants . . . If the synagogues burn today, the churches will be on fire tomorrow.'

As he thought and prayed and agonized in his prison cell, Bonhoeffer came to realize that it was likely he would not survive the war. His final poem, 'The Death of Moses', looked forward in hope to a country and a church committed to justice. He saw the psalms as litmus paper, detecting God's will. He hoped for churches which cared for the disadvantaged. In twenty-first-century terms, his questions are about treatment of refugees, asylum seekers, the growing gap between the rich and the poor. Looking at the churches as institutions, Bonhoeffer's agenda in our new century would ask whether the churches are offering equal opportunities as employers when women are denied many forms of ministry.

Bonhoeffer was also a disciple of community. It seems as though he discovered the value of small communities of Christians in the same way that many Roman Catholics have discovered the Bible in our own days. For him the opportunities for growth and action of a close-knit group inspire one of his most valuable small works, *Life Together* – a practical and profound guide.

Bonhoeffer spent three years as Principal and creator of the Theological College at Finkenwalde, near Stettin in East Prussia. This was the one occasion when the Confessing Church entrusted him with leadership; at least, partially entrusted him with leadership, as it appointed a second-in-command to act as critic and contrast. His task was to guide a Christian community who could live out the Sermon on the Mount under intense pressure. In his own words, 'the real battle must be simply believing endurance . . . I believe that the whole thing will be resolved through the Sermon on the Mount'. His addresses, *Life Together* and *Temptation*, and his book *The Cost of Discipleship* give the flavour of this community life. He had seen National Socialism as an attempt to make history without God. His community was to swim against the stream of the politics and the Church order of Germany, where obedience to the State was customary in the Lutheran Church.

The college began by assembling 20–30 theological students at a disused semi-derelict country house. They renovated the house and collected furniture. They had to beg for their food supplies and they were strongly supported by the old country houses and the large estates of the Prussian military aristocracy in Pomerania. It was all very exciting. There was a lot of laughter and happiness. Within the first fortnight they had been given two grand pianos and, with the customary German musical ability, established a small orchestra. Dietrich Bonhoeffer brought his own very large library from Berlin, and the college started work. It must have felt much like the communities to be formed later at Iona or Taizé. Some Anglican theological colleges after the war, such as Wells and Lincoln, adopted some of Bonhoeffer's ideas.

After considerable struggles with the community, Bonhoeffer persuaded them to spend half an hour a day in meditation. The idea of silent reading of the Bible was very strange, and the students frequently protested. Sometimes the half hour became a corporate time of Bible study and meditation together. Bonhoeffer was anticipating the time when so many of his students would have to be alone either in the army or in prison. He insisted on this severe and, to many of his students, illogical practice of assembling them all in one room to be silent together, as a vital discipline. Always threatened by the State authorities, the college concentrated its work into six months for each group of students. It cared too for depressed and dispirited parishes, and links were maintained with students after they left Finkenwalde. Altogether 300 students were trained, of whom 75 died in action or were executed. Bonhoeffer developed the approach of English trainers of clergy such as Edward King and B. K. Cunningham, and began to write personally to all his former students scattered in the army or in parishes. When the college was closed Bonhoeffer himself ceased to be a pastor. He was employed in the German security forces within the army – and became a member of the conspiracy against Hitler. Ironically, he then found it easier to communicate with his students. The letters he received in return frequently testified to the importance of the secret discipline of meditation, as he called it. Some of his students in 1941 and 1942 were caught in the desperate battles of the invasion of Russia and the Russian winter. Some were in units which were ordered to shoot Russian prisoners and Russian civilians. The attempt to maintain faith and integrity under these horrific conditions drew upon the hidden spiritual discipline which had been learned at Finkenwalde, sustained individually and secretly under the most terrible conditions. Many faced execution for conscience' sake.

Finkenwalde also involved training in the practice of mutual confession and it was through his own confession to Eberhard Bethge, one of his students, that Bonhoeffer himself made one of his deepest friendships. Bethge afterwards married Bonhoeffer's niece and their correspondence when Bethge was fighting in Italy provides the best clues to Bonhoeffer's own thinking at the very end of his life just before his execution. The community spirit which Bonhoeffer developed at the college never cramped the individual growth of its members. In practice it strengthened their individuality. He trained men to be alone with themselves as well as to be open and trusting. He was, at so many points, determined to make the individual free, strong and mature, and not weak or dependent. He believed that

Christ himself, so close to his disciples at every point, was strengthening their personalities.

Dietrich Bonhoeffer, the disciple of community, has a message for us today. The ability to learn from close relations, friends and fellow-workers, enables self-realization. Institutions, especially if they are large and complex, like modern industrial companies, universities or churches, including cathedrals and parishes, can often hinder openness and friendship. By their very busyness, old-fashioned management techniques can keep us at a superficial and impersonal level. In schools, if teachers do not actually like their pupils and listen to them, and in cities, if citizens do not enjoy each other, then all the media marvels of today will fail to bring us together. Empathy dies unless we value all that we can learn through the smaller communities and neighbourhoods. Training in community and our secret discipline of prayer for each other are needed, so that we can each have the vision that 'the world is charged with the grandeur of God'.

The last days of Bonhoeffer in April 1945 were described in the words of a fellow prisoner, Payne Best, a British officer who was held with a group of other very distinguished and, from the Nazi point of view, very dangerous prisoners. Most were Catholic, some Protestant, one from Communist Russia. Low Sunday dawned. The prisoners asked for a service and under general pressure Bonhoeffer yielded. He gave an explanation of the Scripture passages for the day: 'Through his stripes we are healed' (Isaiah 53.5, RSV). 'Blessed be the God and Father of our Lord Jesus Christ, which according to his abundant mercy hath begotten us again unto a lively hope by the resurrection of Jesus Christ from the dead' (1 Peter 1.3, AV). Payne Best says:

He reached the hearts of us all, finding just the right words to express the spirit of our imprisonment and the thoughts and resolutions which it had brought. The little service ended. Then, during the moment of stillness that succeeded it, the door was flung open and two men stood in the doorway. 'Prisoner Bonhoeffer, get ready and come with us,' one of them said. Bonhoeffer gathered his few belongings. He had a copy of Plutarch that he had received for his birthday. He put his name in it in large letters and left it on the table.

His last words to Payne Best were a message to his trusted English friend, Bishop Bell of Chichester. 'Tell him that for me this is the end, but also the beginning. With him I believe in the principle of our universal Christian brotherhood which rises above all national interests and that our victory is certain. Tell him, too, that I have never forgotten his words at our last meeting.' The last sight of Bonhoeffer was in his prison clothes kneeling in fervent prayer to the Lord his God.

> The devout and evident conviction of being heard that I saw in the prayer of this intensely captivating man moved me to the depths. So the morning came. The prisoners had to strip. They were led down a little flight of steps under the trees to the secluded place of execution. There was a pause. For the men about to die, time hung a moment suspended. Naked under the scaffold in the sweet spring woods, Bonhoeffer knelt for the last time to pray. Five minutes later, his life was ended.
> (See Eberhard Bethge, *Dietrich Bonhoeffer*, pp. 829ff.)

Had Bonhoeffer been a painter, he might have adopted Vincent van Gogh's words, when he said that the time had come 'to paint saints not with haloes outside and around their head, but actually within their characters, inside their eyes'. It was Bonhoeffer's conviction that the reality of God in God's fullness, with all his holiness, all his transcendent majesty, all his utter self-sacrifice for humanity seen in the crucifixion of his Son, is found within the divine spirit which lives within every human being. Bonhoeffer knew the ambiguities of life. He yearned in prison for the companionship of the woman to whom he had become engaged. He suffered many anxieties. But when the air-raids came, especially in burning Berlin, and the pressures were at their highest, he managed to be firm and steadfast. As we see in Martin Luther King and other martyrs of the past 100 years, he was not a perfect Christian. He had helped to plan a murder. He was a disciple prepared to pay the cost, prepared to live in community, a disciple who tried to be both for others and for God.

Bonhoeffer looked forward to a 'world come of age', when humanity would find God in its strengths – scientific achievement and an international sense of justice and human rights. He insisted that believers should not fear secularization because prayer, the communion of saints and courageous faith would be as valid as ever. God is always hidden. The Christian task is not the strengthening of churches as established institutions but a growth in ecumenism, understanding other faiths and a deepening of personal relationships. The struggle against injustice and selfishness would continue to demand the courage of Christians in deeds, not only in words. He was reaching for reality in religion and for this he gave his life.

References

Bethge, Eberhard, *Dietrich Bonhoeffer*. London, Collins, 1970.
Chandler, Andrew, ed., *The Terrible Alternative*. London, Cassell, 1998.
Robertson, Edwin, *Voices in the Night*. Grand Rapids, Michigan, Zondervan, 1999.

9 MOTHER JULIAN AND DIVINE LOVE

The catastrophes of the twentieth century have made it hard for people to be religious in the old sense. In Christendom it has become impossible to rely on the old religious authorities. The Holocaust and the two world wars proved our structures, political and religious, had been found wanting. Inevitably the authorities in religion were no longer the established powerful structures of the churches but the martyrs and those on the fringes. The divine spirit within our own minds, hearts, wills and consciences became questioning, even subversive.

Our children and grandchildren will still find moments when their personal experience of love, and their experience of caring for others, will be fed from the story of Jesus Christ, perhaps through prayer, Bible reading, sacraments and many forms of worship, using the resources of music, art and drama. Their concern for integrity in relationships and for care and justice for the vulnerable may be as demanding as the work of missionaries in earlier centuries. They may use the words of the Lord's Prayer 'Your kingdom come' and mean those words with the determination of a Bonhoeffer and the other martyrs of the last century.

In this ambiguous culture religion may grow from below rather than in organized churches, sometimes felt to be exclusive, cosy and less imaginative than the outside world. It may become normal to move in and out of churches and to allow faith to develop and change as the decades pass. But as we experience doubt and agnosticism it matters that the divine presence should be benign, not leading to a culture of blaming others or ourselves. 'Almighty' can be one of the most misleading of all words used to describe God, as if God was in essence an angry judge and had encouraged the Crusades, the Inquisition and the religious intolerance from which so many independent thinkers have suffered. The wisest guides may be those on the fringe, least concerned with the Establishment or the creation of impressive dogmatic edifices. The unsung contemporary workers in the world's famine areas, struggling to recreate trust and self-esteem after natural disaster or genocide, or in Britain social indifference, may be the religious gurus of the future.

We need voices from the fringe who risk speaking of God, wonderful beyond words, deep within us all, the caring and vitalizing love which flows through humanity. One crucial pioneering fringe thinker for today, recently rediscovered, both subversive and creative, is Julian of Norwich.

Her book, *Revelations of Divine Love*, was the first attempt in English to describe a God without anger and to construct an image of a consistently compassionate God. Others before Julian had written theology but they had written in Latin for the learned. Then on 8 May 1373, Julian had an extraordinary experience against a background of personal illness. Perhaps she was a widow who had lost a child in the appalling Black Death. Her times were disturbed by the Peasants' Revolt and violent disputes in the church between the bishops and John Wyclif. She lived beside St Julian's Church in the city of Norwich, and took her name from that church, already an ancient place of prayer. She described God within us, sharing our suffering and our joy – infinite empathy. As she grew older her metaphors for God became more homely, more anchored in reality.

Chaucer and others had written in English just before her, but hers is the first book written by a woman in English. The heart of her theology was the conviction that our Lord is to us everything that is good, and comforting for our help. 'He is our clothing, for he is that love which wraps and enfolds us, embraces us and guides us, surrounds us ... And so in this sight I saw truly that he is everything that is good ... He is the ground of our praying ...'

Learned men are still astonished that a woman should be our first theologian writing in English. Julian has in many ways been ignored. She does not appear in the relevant volumes of the Oxford History of England. More surprisingly, *The Oxford Illustrated History of*

Christianity, published in 1990, does not mention Julian. But her hour is coming. In 1979 the new American prayer book gave her a day in the calendar (8 May) as did the *Alternative Service Book 1980* in England and *Common Worship* in 2000. There is now a Julian community in America, and in this country there are hundreds of small groups, mainly lay people, meeting regularly for contemplative prayer – praying together in silence. In 1999 there were more than 400 Julian groups in the UK alone.

Thomas Merton said: 'She gets greater and greater in my eyes, as I grow older'. Richard Harries, Bishop of Oxford, has wondered whether she might be 'the greatest woman this country has produced'. She grips us because she is writing about our own identity, the mystery of personality and its link with the divine Spirit. There is something of the divine in us and, through Jesus Christ, humanity is in God.

Churches have hesitated to grant leadership to women. In both the Roman Catholic and the Orthodox Church women are still forbidden to be priests though in both churches, particularly the Roman Catholic, there is a growing body of opinion in support of women's ordination. Julian has shown that a woman can be among the most perceptive and balanced of religious guides. Perhaps when women are everywhere welcomed as bishops, priests, theologians and pastors and given full responsibility in the churches, new insights may further the gospel. Today change is once again on the agenda of the churches and women may be the midwives of the new birth. Certainly fresh starts are being made, earthed and rooted in reality. Of Julian, Archbishop Michael Ramsey said, 'She was not a "visionary", as she saw the things of God through the medium of human life itself, as experienced in a time of suffering and frustration.'

To mark her anniversary in May 1973 there was an international and ecumenical Eucharist in Norwich Cathedral, which created changed perceptions for the churches. New anthems and hymns were composed, stressing the primacy of love and the assurance that God is with us all. The 1973 festival emphasized what is universal in religion. The East Anglian sunlight with its sparkling clarity enhanced the joy of those who came. The French and English nuns and sisters gathered rose petals flung down by young people in the clerestories high above them, and put them in their missals, as if they were at a wedding. A Jesuit preached, a Methodist Chairman of District concelebrated, and an Anglican and a Roman Catholic bishop, though they were not able to receive the sacrament, gave the blessing together. It felt as though the quarrels of centuries had been reconciled in shared and joyful prayer.

Ten years later at the instigation of Bishop Kenneth Woollcombe on 8 May 1983, St Paul's Cathedral invited Roman Catholic and Anglican religious to join in worship together. Five hundred religious came, joined by hundreds of lay people, and processed together out of the cathedral to St Paul's Cross for the blessing. That evening the Movement for the Ordination of Women, which drew inspiration from Julian, held a service in the crypt of St Paul's. These and other services celebrating Julian of Norwich stressed the need for unity and compassion, and brought divided Christians together. The study of her theology questions the divisiveness that leads to the refusal to share sacraments.

The Julian cell in Norwich has been the scene of reconciliation of wartime enemies. A year after the 600th celebration in Norwich, two men, one of whom was guiding his friend who was blind, came quietly and privately to the Rouen Road church beside which Julian had lived – a modern reconstruction as the original church was destroyed by an air raid in World War II. It is quiet and many visit it to pause and pray. The blind man was led in to the small dark cell through the church. He had been a prisoner of war under the Japanese and his blindness was partly a result of the harsh treatment he had received. The two men knelt together in silence. Then the blind man believed that he actually saw Julian, and standing with her the Japanese soldier responsible for his suffering, who had died after the war. He believed that the dead Japanese soldier had been brought to ask forgiveness. The blind Englishman burst into a torrent of vehement Japanese and then suddenly felt released from resentment, and his denunciation broke into an ecstasy of joy. The two men then went to the convent guesthouse next door, where one of the Sisters gave them tea. During tea, the blind man poured out his heart in great animation, again in Japanese. No one else saw anything, but the blind man went away reconciled and understanding the purpose of his

journey to Julian's cell; he could think of his terrible hardships 'with
pity, not with blame'. He died a year or two later. (Quoted from
R. Llewelyn, *With Pity Not With Blame*, 1982.)

The writings and prayers of Julian have inspired many more
twentieth-century reconciliations. Julian prayer groups in homes,
and Julian retreats, which draw inspiration from her theological
approach, bring together Christians from different churches. I have
experienced at the Irish School of Ecumenics in Dublin, and at
Hengrave Hall in Suffolk, how Catholics and Protestants can work
and pray together, finding in Julian a remarkable level of spiritual
agreement and going to work together for human justice and compassion. In Boston, Massachusetts, Trinity Church in 1993 arranged
an evening weekday lecture for hundreds of lay people with the
same intention and the same consequence.

Like many pioneers Julian was modest about herself. John Keats
once said that the finest poetry should be 'great and unobtrusive';
Julian was remarkably unobtrusive and in her days women were not
thought competent to teach. Her message was nearly lost. Only one
copy of the first shorter version of *Revelations of Divine Love* and three
copies of the longer version she wrote 20 years later survive. She is
merely mentioned in several wills, but like other anchoresses she was
regarded as a 'wise woman', worth consulting because she had shared
so many contemporary hardships and tragedies. Margery Kempe of
King's Lynn has left long accounts of their talks together, and Julian
herself describes conversations with her mother, her priest and other
friends.

Julian's Thinking and Environment

In medieval Norwich there were about 30 or 40 religious women
living a solitary, literally enclosed, life of prayer, counselling and
writing, enjoying the good will of the Church and the citizens. It
was a fringe religious movement – not spiritually satisfied by the
authoritarian and regulated life of monasteries and nunneries, or for
that matter by the Cathedral or the Bishop – in Julian's time Henry
Despenser, who led his troops in person. Relatives and friends supported them and they often received grants from wills – occasionally

getting into trouble with the authorities, for instance for failing to arrange the clearance of their garbage from the streets. Perhaps Julian's room had three windows, one into the Chapel, one into the kitchen, and one into the outside world, through which she conversed. A map of medieval Norwich shows the anchorite cells scattered evenly throughout the city inside the walls. The Norwich motto is 'Do Different', and Norwich was a seed bed for fresh religious and social ideas and later a natural home for Protestant refugees from Europe and other radical groups, both religious and political. Ecclesiastical authorities struggled unsuccessfully to control dissent.

Julian's *Revelations* began by meditating on the vulnerability of Christ, his passion, suffering and the crown of thorns. She imagined herself with Christ and prayed that she might share his sufferings in her own illness. Julian felt the blood of Christ pouring over her, copious as a shower of rain; the drops as large as herring scales. She seemed to experience in a profound and appalling way the reality of watching the crucifixion, as she lay so seriously ill.

The *Revelations of Divine Love* continue with the parable of the hazelnut.

And he showed me something small, no bigger than a hazelnut, lying in the palm of my hand, and I perceived that it was round like a ball. I looked at it and thought: 'What can this be?' and I was given this general answer: 'It is everything that is made'. I was amazed that it could last, for I thought that it was so small that it could suddenly fall into nothing. And I was answered in my understanding: 'It lasts and always will, because God loves it; and thus everything has being through the love of God'. In this little thing I saw three properties. The first is that God made it; the second is that he loves it; the third is that God preserves it. But what is that to me? It is that God is the creator and the lover and the protector. For until I am substantially united to him, I can never have love or rest or true happiness; until, that is, I am so attached to him that there can be no created thing between my God and me. And who will do this thing? Truly, he himself, by his mercy and his grace, for he has made me for this and has blessedly restored me.

Julian saw planet Earth enfolded in the love of God. In our days the astronauts, coming back from the moon, saw a small multi-coloured planet and took their famous photograph. Julian linked together the assurance that we are loved by God, the delight we ought to have in the creation, and the feeling of sharing God's creative love and the sense that we are with God, not primarily through obedience or because we are afraid of him, or even because we respect his wisdom, but simply by love. This is an image similar to Teilhard de Chardin's vision of the Coming Christ who in some mysterious way brings loving care to the evolving thought of our planet.

Someone who is disorientated or has been the victim of violence or rape or deep depression may feel, 'I hate my body. It is dirty, unclean, shameful and revolting'. Many women and men who have suffered abuse, perhaps within their family circles, experience a sense of the inadequacy of their bodies, and even come to hate their bodies. The profound parable of the hazelnut – that fragile things, like our bodies, exist because they are held in the loving hand of God, that we are clothed and given extraordinary value by God's love – is relevant and therapeutic. (See Brian Thorne, *Person Centred Counselling*, 1991.)

The fragility of planet Earth, the fragility of our acceptance of ourselves and our short lives, all this evokes from Julian – herself at this time desperately sick – the conviction that we are carried, clothed, loved by God. Like St Francis, she realized the implications for our attitude to nature. As the law of gravity controls movement in planet Earth, so the reality of God's love gives worth and assurance to every living thing, including the environment where we live. In the luminous words of a Roman Catholic conference at San Domingo in 1992, 'Land is life, a holy place, the feminine face of God.'

When she reconsidered her religious experience for the later Longer Version, probably in 1393, she re-imagined this conviction about the divine love. The Gospels had already hinted that God regards us with that maternal love with which a hen guards her chickens (Matthew 23.37; Luke 13.34). St Anselm, another sensitive English theologian, had spoken of God as mother. Julian carried this further, and spoke both of God and our Lord Jesus Christ as mother as well as father as well as brother. God forgives us whatever we do, like the wise human mother. God is not primarily judgemental or moralistic but primarily accepting. As Professor Brian Thorne has put it: 'Mother Julian of Norwich would have it that the helper shares in the parenthood of God as he or she offers unconditional acceptance to the client, and that is saying something very big indeed.' Sister Elizabeth Ruth Obbard in her Julian Lecture for 2000 described Julian as a 'woman in transition' who knew 'the God of the second chance'.

Christendom often reacts to wickedness, injustice, cruelty and suffering by portraying God in judgement. Many of the vivid East Anglian dooms, those paintings of the Last Judgement which confronted worshippers each Sunday, were erected in her lifetime. The valour of the Crusaders, and the rigour of church courts in suppressing heresy, emphasized God as judge. Julian took the risk of insisting that God suffers. For God the 'injustice' of forgiveness is wiser and more effective than the sentences of human justice.

Christ's parables sometimes shock by their teaching of what looks like weak forgiveness, cheap grace and irrational sentimentality. The elder brother in the parable of the prodigal son, the labourers who worked all day, the righteous Pharisees all had legitimate grievances. Human society requires justice, equity and if necessary penalties. But these are secondary values in contrast to the absolute love and mercy of a constantly forgiving and suffering God. Julian taught that God forgives before we repent, is loving while we are still angry. God does not blame us but works to release us from the aggression and self-hatred that can dominate our characters. Julian lived through personal, social and material sufferings and bitter disputes. She did not blame God or man, church or state, her city or her community. For her it was a settled conviction that a loving, suffering God could win us to repentance and even felicity, through his absolute compassion and unimaginable love.

Julian returned again and again to her faith that we can have the same confidence in ourselves, in our bodies and personalities, as children have when in the hands of a welcoming and loving mother. 'The human mother may put her child tenderly to her breast, but our tender Mother Jesus simply leads us into his blessed breast through his open side, and there gives us a glimpse of the Godhead and heavenly joy – the inner certainty of eternal bliss.' And she goes on:

> This fine and lovely word 'Mother' is so sweet, and so much its own, that it cannot properly be used of any but him, and of her who is his own true Mother – and ours. In essence *motherhood* means love and kindness, wisdom, knowledge, goodness.

Her emphasis on motherhood and goodness did not mean that she shut her eyes to sin. Sin, she wrote, was 'behovely', by which she meant needful, necessary, or useful. Tyndale was to write that Christ's death was 'behovely'. Like George Herbert or Thomas Traherne centuries later, she saw God's children as blessed by God's love rather than broken by divine anger.

Julian of Norwich reminded Brian Thorne of one of William Blake's most tragic poems, 'The Garden of Love', where he reflects on the gloom and negativity of so much church thinking on sexuality:

> And I saw it was filled with graves,
> And tombstones where flowers should be;
> And Priests in black gowns were walking their rounds
> And binding with briars my joys and desires.

Julian, like Blake, pleaded with the Church not to see sensuality as something to be condemned or feared or punished, but rather to allow the overflowing divine love to heal and enlighten. In practice the Church has often been condemnatory and gloom laden, speaking more of sin than of the blessings and happiness God would have us share.

Julian on the other hand thought about the centre of faith, the flowing love from God to humanity; that within every human personality there is a central core, beloved by God, which has not sinned; the old view that God was angry was not true. When she was challenged, perhaps by her parish priest, that the Bible and the Church taught that God was angry about human sin, that the wrath of God was recorded in Scripture, she replied that she was sure that

God was not angry, 'but the meaning shall be clear hereafter'. She left her convictions to be justified in eternity.

She was clear that her teaching was not to divide Christians, and she insisted that she was not against the teaching of the Church. Her theological integrity required her to challenge church teaching that the God we worship is primarily an angry God. Julian insisted that the core of Christianity was that 'all shall be well, and all shall be well, and all manner of thing shall be well'; that sin was behovely, it was a necessity of human life, but it was always secondary.

Julian did not believe that our petitions are always granted but that prayer creates a new relationship.

> Our Lord wants us both to pray and to trust . . . for he wants us to be certain that our prayers are answered because prayer pleases God. Prayers make a praying man pleased with himself and make the man serious and humble, who before this was contending and striving against himself.

Prayer unites the soul to God and so God teaches us to pray and have firm trust. She longed for us to be at home, or at ease with ourselves, not on an ego trip but happy that we are partners with God. We share the loving spirit, we can ask for no more, the soul is united to God. In prayer God says, 'I am glad that you have found rest for I have always loved you and I love you now and you love me.' When the soul is tempted and troubled in its unrest, that is the time for it to pray and to make itself supple. Prayer is a school of loving and growing in pleasure with God and acceptance of oneself.

Julian stressed the limitations of our knowledge. She recounted how she wished to know the answer to a prayer for someone else, and was told that she would not be given the answer. It is as if she heard that wise advice not to press in religion. Pray as you can and not as you can't. You will not know the answers but you can grow in empathy and love and care. If God is the ground of our praying and the Divine is within us, then in the silence God is there. Much grief, much business, many wandering thoughts do not block our approach to God. In the act of praying we realize that God has been with us from our birth. Praying is the bringing to consciousness of what is always everywhere true. Julian said we might be 'tempest-tossed but not overcome'.

Julian's Language and Symbolism

Those who have studied the language of Julian's praying point to the use of the words 'homely' and 'courtesy' and the number of her illustrations from daily life. In the story she tells (in the Longer Version) of the Lord and the servant who falls into a ditch and suffers so much, it is significant that the Lord gives time for the servant to speak when he comes to rescue him. The courtesy of relationships in religion requires that we should wait for the other to speak, and not thrust our convictions until the other asks us. This courtesy is essential when Christians, Hindus, Muslims, Buddhists and Jews speak to each other. Julian was always aware that we need to communicate the all-supporting grace of God, rather than proclaim our own truths to others, still less try to make them feel guilty.

Perhaps her description of walking at the bottom of the sea was an analogy from swimming on the North Norfolk coast, in shallow water. She realized that the water supports every part of the body, as if to say that all our faculties – mind and sensuality – are supported by the loving grace of God, not threatened or pressurized or violently penetrated. God's approach is persuasive, a gentle waiting, a discreet acknowledgement of ourselves. It is a relationship not a manipulation; God, like water in swimming, is always with us.

> If I take the wings of the morning
> and dwell in the uttermost parts of the sea,
> even there shall thy hand lead me,
> and thy right hand shall hold me.
> (Psalm 139.9–10, RSV)

Julian had special reasons for asking whether God is always with us. To be an anchorite meant you were withdrawn from normal life. Julian had been walled up after a religious ceremony like a funeral, taken by the bishop. She could never again, in her whole life, leave her cell. This sounds horrifically cruel, and no doubt there could be intense depression. However, there were humane compensations for the anchoress. Her cell would be three or four rooms attached to a church; most anchoresses had one or two servants and some kept a cow and most a cat. (Their Rule discussed the difficulties and dangers of keeping cows in the centre of a city with narrow streets and crowded housing.) Keeping fit was remembered in the Rule and they were urged to feed themselves properly. They could go for a walk in the churchyard, if there was one. They were respected in the community and enjoyed a rare freedom from sexual harassment.

Anchorites were counsellors, much visited for advice, personal and spiritual, admired for following the path of Mary in contrast to Martha. With time for prayer and considering the needs of others, they were consulted by the wealthy as well as by the poor: even, in one case at Westminster, by the king himself, at a time of special tension. Their confidentiality is stressed in their Rule; as the years went by they became more knowledgeable about relationships within the community and evidently the powerful and cynical valued someone who would listen and pray and enable them to plead for the mercy of God. But all this could only be sustained if they remained confident that God's love was constant.

At the heart of Julian's understanding of Christianity is the concept of personal relationship; not two separate bodies talking over a divide but the divine within the human. For Julian, love flows between God and humanity, a love verified in the sharing of the pain of the Cross.

Julian was precise about how we should grow in love and prayer.

Flee to our Lord and we shall be comforted. Touch him and we shall be made clean. Cling to him and we shall be safe and sound from every kind of danger. For our courteous Lord wills that we should be as at home with him as heart may think or soul may desire ... I saw no whit of anger in God in short or in long term ... God looks upon us with pity, not with blame.

At times when we let ourselves down and fail our own standards we can be self-destructive. Julian said, 'In your eyes you do not stand.

In God's eyes you do not fall. I see both to be true, but God's insight is the deeper one.' Here Julian was warning against an over-rigid ego, which suffers when things change. We cling to the old order, defend ourselves when threatened by change, and have an itch for perfection. Julian was quite unusually free in her willingness to talk about the bodily earthy aspects of humanity. As one of her admirers has said, 'What other mystic has used as an example of the wonder of God's creating love the fact that a man walks upright and the food in his body is shut in as in a well-made purse. When the time of his necessity comes, the purse is opened and shut again in most seemly fashion.'

Julian was not over-nice. She understood the dirtiness and worries of human life. She tells a story.

> I saw a body lying on the earth which appeared heavy and horrible and without shape and form, as it were a swollen pit of stinking mud, and suddenly out of this body there sprang a most beautiful creature, a little child, fully shaped and formed, swift and lively and whiter than a lily, which quickly glided up to heaven ... it is more blissful that man be taken from pain than pain be taken from man, for if pain be taken away from us it may come again.

Perhaps she was describing the death of her own child in the plague, and the sense that pain comes back again and again. In her thinking about the Cross she became convinced that God himself suffers pain, and has taken pain into himself through Jesus Christ. She heard Christ say that if he could have suffered more for us, he would. In her mind's eye she saw Christ's feet, not snowy white as in a church window, but covered with the dust and dirt of the roads of Palestine. Her Christ is earthy.

It is also significant, as Grace Jantzen has pointed out, that she never mentioned chastity. No doubt some time in her life she took the vow, but she never linked chastity or celibacy with godliness. Her silence is eloquent and very different from Margery Kempe, who talked of the 'stains of marriage' as a barrier to wholehearted love. Perhaps Julian had renounced sexual activity but she does not spend time discussing it. For her, love flowed to and from God. She had no self-loathing, no suggestion that women are lower than men in the sight of God. Julian longed that believers should experience a sense of self-worth. For her it was more important that we believe that God loves us, not that he requires us to be chaste.

In the past the churches have emphasized our sins and God's anger. Today, when immense energy is given to competitive monetarism, or to maximizing the arms trade, it is more vital than ever that we should share in a revelation of divine love. Humanity must love Planet Earth instead of ravishing and raping it. Julian was vividly attentive to the detail of what she saw and heard around her. She grasped the significance of the tiny hazelnut, saw symbolism in the washing hung outside her house, and in the shores around the Norfolk coast.

She was both down to earth and visionary in her writing about delight and laughter.

> Glad and merry and sweet is the blessed and lovely demeanour of our Lord towards our souls, for he saw us always living in love, and he wants our souls to be gladly disposed towards him, to repay him is to reward. And so I hope that by his grace he lifts up and will draw our outer disposition to our inward, and will make us all at unity with him, and each of us with others in the true lasting joy which is Jesus.

Just as Jesus Christ had spoken of parties and banquets, so she saw Christians being invited to the heavenly feast.

> I saw him reign in his house as a king, and fill it all full of joy and mirth, gladdening and consoling his dear friends with himself very familiarly and courteously, with wonderful melody.

In her imagination she saw Christ with a fair, blissful countenance, and heaven full of the joy and the bliss of the divinity. She hoped that her fellow Christians would share her vision:

> You would know our Lord's meaning? Love was his meaning.

Who showed it to you? Love. Why did he show it? For love. Hold
on to this and you will understand love more and more, but you
will not know or understand anything else ever! . . . Love was our
Lord's meaning, and I saw for certain, that before ever he made
us, God loved us; and that God never slackened, nor ever
shall . . . He did not say 'You shall not be tempest-tossed, you shall
not be work-weary, you shall not be discomforted'. But he said
'You shall not be overcome.' God wants us to heed these words so
that we shall always be strong in trust, both in sorrow and in joy.

Julian's thinking, therefore, was the converse of the theology of God
as an angry, an all-powerful judge. 'Provoking most justly thy wrath
and indignation against us' is still said in some churches, influencing
our subconscious. Church leaders who urge gentleness are
denounced as wimps, Robert Runcie is criticized for praying for
enemy Argentinian dead and David Jenkins for defending unemployed miners from harsh redundancies.

The rediscovery of Julian with her emphasis on acceptance, not
guilt, hope not certainty has been liberating for Christians. Instead
of insisting on a literal adherence to ancient scriptures and creeds,
she urged that through prayer we experience God's presence with us
now and in the future. This is a faith that our world, our churches
and our relationships can all be guided by the Spirit of God, a spirit
like that of wise and loving parents, both Father and Mother. Then
indeed, to quote Julian's most famous insight, 'All shall be well, and
all shall be well, and all manner of thing shall be well'.

O Spirit of God, breathe into us
such strong affection and such homely wisdom,
that taught by your servant Julian,
we may know that your hands hold all:
Grant us to live without despair or anger,
and to worship you as our father and mother,
shining your goodness in every single thing.
This we pray through your dear son, Jesus Christ our Lord.
(Prayer used at Julian 1973 celebrations)

References

Jantzen, Grace, *Julian of Norwich*. London, SPCK, 1987. This outstanding study is especially significant for those concerned with prayer, psychotherapy and counselling.

Julian of Norwich, *Revelations of Divine Love* translated by Clifton Wolters. Harmondsworth, Penguin, 1966.

[Another translation:] *Showings*, translated from the critical text with an introduction by Edmund Colledge and James Walsh. New York, Paulist Press, 1978.

[Selections:] *Enfolded in Love: Daily Readings with Julian of Norwich*, editor Robert Llewelyn, assistant editor Michael McLean, translated by Sheila Upjohn. London, Darton, Longman & Todd, 1999.

Julian of Norwich, an introduction. All Hallows, Ditchingham, 1996.

Llewelyn, Robert, *Love Bade Me Welcome*. London, Darton, Longman & Todd, 1984.

Llewelyn, Robert, *Memories and Reflections*. London, Darton, Longman & Todd, 1998. Robert Llewelyn was for many years Guardian of the Julian Shrine in Norwich, and to his friendship I owe much of my understanding of Julian.

Llewelyn, Robert, *With Pity Not with Blame: Reflections on the Writings of Julian of Norwich and on The Cloud of Unknowing*. London, Darton, Longman & Todd, 1982.

Obbard, Elizabeth Ruth, *Julian: a Woman in Transition*. Norwich, Julian Shrine, 2000.

Sayer, Frank, ed., *Julian and her Norwich: Commemorative Essays and Handbook to the Exhibition 'Revelations of Divine Love'*. Norwich, 1973.

Upjohn, Sheila, *In Search of Julian of Norwich*. London, Darton, Longman & Todd, 1989.

Upjohn, Sheila, *Why Julian Now? A Voyage of Discovery*. London, Darton, Longman & Todd, 1997.

Ward, Benedicta, 'Lady Julian of Norwich and her Audience: "Mine Even-Christian"' in *The English Religious Tradition and the Genius of Anglicanism* edited by Geoffrey Rowell. Wantage, Ikon, 1992.

Webster, Alan, *Suffering: the Jews of Norwich and Julian of Norwich*. London Diocesan Council for Christian–Jewish Understanding, 1981 (St Paul's Lecture).

For the 1973 celebration of the 600th anniversary, Fred Pratt Green, the Methodist hymn-writer and poet, contributed a memorable hymn 'Rejoice in God's Saints', and Alan Wilson composed an anthem from Julian's words, 'My Faith is a Light'. In 1982, St Paul's Cathedral commissioned an anthem from William Mathias, 'As Truly as God is our Father, so just as Truly is He our Mother'.

Many books by and about Julian are available at All Hallows House, Rouen Road, Norwich NR1 1PE.

Information on Julian Meetings is available from The Rectory, Kingstone, Hereford HR2 9EY, and on the Internet at www.julianmeetings.org

10 AND SO . . . ?

In his foreword Ronald Blythe writes of the different perceptions of the past century. He describes these years as 'both the most appalling and the most scientifically progressive in human history'. Granted that some saw it as simply 'post-Christian' or 'secular' still there were times and events of a 'profoundly religious nature'. Some of the century's most impressive characters, perceptive thinkers and self-sacrificial campaigners for justice had religious motivations. It is reasonable to ask, 'What are the wells of hope for our successors in the religious world in the twenty-first century?'

Unobtrusive but crucial in sustaining hope are those individuals who give themselves for a better world and campaign personally and publicly for justice in human life. The last century has bequeathed us a tradition which will continue to challenge and enable. One example, tucked away in the calendar of the prayer book of the American Episcopal Church, is one of the forgotten student heroes of the much-criticized sixties. Under the date 14 August is the name Jonathan Daniels (1939–65).

Daniels shared experiences common amongst post war student generations, especially in America, France and England. Should he give himself to law, medicine, writing or ordination? His New England and Harvard background left him at times agnostic, at other times mildly church-going. Then the Easter service at a Boston parish church and the community experience in a Cambridge, Mass. theological college, led him to respond to Martin Luther King's televised appeal for help in the civil rights campaign. His calling had been deepened by words at Evening Prayer during the singing of the Magnificat: 'He hath put down the mighty from their seat and hath exalted the humble and meek. He hath filled the hungry with good things.' So he travelled to the South, and there put himself in front of a 17-year-old student, threatened by a deputy sheriff's gun, and on the top step of the entrance to a small Selma store in Alabama, he received the blast which killed him.

One of Daniels' cruel discoveries at Selma was that his own church in that Southern town did not welcome him or his friends at worship, still less support giving the vote to black citizens. Churches who have been blind to injustice need the army of activists who act as pathfinders.

These pathfinders are more adventurous than their parent churches. Arriving in El Salvador during its costly civil war, under the auspices of Christian Aid, the Catholic Institute for International Affairs and the Free Churches' inspired Action for Central America, I was immediately asked by the Roman Catholic Franciscan Sisters to lead their worship, an invitation which would not have been made in the UK. In the twenty-first century the multitude of voluntary bodies who care for every kind of human need, whether Samaritans, Amnesty International, Médecins sans Frontières or Voluntary Service Overseas, are signs of hope. Governments, churches, cities and the media take notice.

Another sign of hope arises from the new millennium's huge expansion in scientific research and discovery. Never has the relationship with science and the culture which it has created been so important for religion. It is encouraging that some universities, foundations and research institutions are now giving attention to the interface of religion, science and the humanities. The influential Templeton Foundation for encouraging 'progress in religion' awarded its prize in 2001 to Arthur Peacocke who, as a physical biochemist, made DNA-related discoveries. He is also a theologian, having become ordained after hearing the preaching of William Temple. Other scientists writing in the area of religion and science, Paul Davies and Freeman Dyson, have received the Templeton Prize. Stephen Jay Gould from the standpoint of an agnostic Jew has argued that 'people of goodwill wish to see science and religion at peace'. The outlooks of these thinkers differ and the search for a common philosophy will be long, but the reconciliation of science and religion is now receiving attention around the world. Food and botanical research institutions are this century's response to the dream of the Magnificat that 'He hath filled the hungry with good things'. The nightmares of chemical, biological or nuclear warfare or the excesses of human engineering need to give way to a caring sacrificial society.

At the beginning of the millennium another refreshing change, ultimately as significant for the churches as those already mentioned, is found in a new approach to the Bible. Many devout Christians in the nineteenth century, including most famously Charles Darwin, left the churches because of the conflict between treating the Bible as objective literal truth and reality as they knew it in the researches of historians and scientists. In the twentieth century those who used the Bible to provide knock-down answers to ethical problems, especially in sexual morality, have not done the Christian community good service. Now we can allow ourselves to see the Bible as it really is, with stories of escape, and triumph and even genocide and the slow growth of the claims of righteousness and mercy. It is not a moral code or an infallible dogmatic treatise or a blueprint for ecclesiastical structures, but has riches far beyond.

The imaginative wonder of the gospel was illustrated when St Mark's Gospel was recently described by an Oxford New Testament scholar, Dr John Fenton, as 'the best book for the twenty-first century because it is so utterly subversive. Western European culture will need some subversive people to do something about its capitalism and its love of self . . . Away success! Welcome failure. That is the good news' (*Theology*, March 2001). No doubt the centuries ahead have much to learn from western philosophy and eastern religions but the utterly godly radical who was described in the earliest Gospel as crying, as he came to die, 'My God, My God, why hast thou forsaken me', will remain at the heart of the human search for meaning.

The hope that the coming centuries will care more for compassion and justice than the centuries which have preceded them often seems a vain hope. Yet the small efforts, described in the preceding pages, to reach towards this hope and convert it into reality have made a tiny contribution to change. The poets and musicians, writers and artists and, for that matter, entertainers and gardeners and cooks also have their own wells of hope and draw refreshment from them. Among those sources of fresh life will be the religious community, relying on the conviction that people are somehow in touch with God, loved and cared for by the divine spirit. Among them will be those who will relive the story of the life, death and resurrection of Jesus Christ, hidden, mysterious but strangely compelling.

The Society for Promoting Christian Knowledge (SPCK) was founded in 1698. Its mission statement is:

To promote Christian knowledge by

- **Communicating the Christian faith in its rich diversity;**
- **Helping people to understand the Christian faith and to develop their personal faith; and**
- **Equipping Christians for mission and ministry.**

SPCK Worldwide serves the Church through Christian literature and communication projects in over 100 countries, and provides books for those training for ministry in many parts of the developing world. This worldwide service depends upon the generosity of others and all gifts are spent wholly on ministry programmes, without deductions.

SPCK Bookshops support the life of the Christian community by making available a full range of Christian literature and other resources, providing support for those training for ministry, and assisting bookstalls and book agents throughout the UK.

SPCK Publishing produces Christian books and resources, covering a wide range of inspirational, pastoral, practical and academic subjects. Authors are drawn from many different Christian traditions, and publications aim to meet the needs of a wide variety of readers in the UK and throughout the world.

The Society does not necessarily endorse the individual views contained in its publications, but hopes they stimulate readers to think about and further develop their Christian faith.

For further information about the Society, visit our website at
www.spck.org.uk, or write to:
SPCK, Holy Trinity Church, Marylebone Road,
London NW1 4DU, United Kingdom.